3-

THE BOY'S BOOK OF VERSE

THE BOY'S BOOK OF VERSE

An Anthology Compiled By

HELEN DEAN FISH

1951 REVISION

J. B. Lippincott Company

PHILADELPHIA AND NEW YORK

Revised Edition
Thirteenth Printing

PRINTED IN THE UNITED STATES OF AMERICA

Library of Congress Catalog Card Number 51-10647

ISBN-0-397-30183-9

ACKNOWLEDGMENTS

Permission to reprint material copyright or controlled by various publishers, agents and individuals has been granted by the following:

YOUNG E. ALLISON for "Derelict."

HENRY H. BENNETT for "The Flag Goes By."

DODD, MEAD AND COMPANY for "Jesse James" and "The Horse Thief" from *The Golden Fleece,* copyright 1927 by William Rose Benét; "At the Crossroads" and lines from "Spring" from *Poems* by Richard Hovey; "Visions" from *My Ship* by Edmund Leamy; "Play the Game," "He Fell Among Thieves," "Hawke" and "The Old Superb" from *Poems New and Old* by Henry Newbolt; "The Coromandel Fishers" from *The Broken Wing* by Sarojini Naidu; "Soldier, What Did You See?" from *Pilot Bails Out,* copyright 1943 by Don Blanding.

DOUBLEDAY AND COMPANY, INC., for Rudyard Kipling's "Ballad of East and West," "Gunga Din" and "Recessional" from *Departmental Ditties and Ballads and Barrack Room Ballads,* and "If" from *Rewards and Fairies,* copyright 1910 by Rudyard Kipling, reprinted by permission of Mrs. George Bambridge and Doubleday and Company, Inc. And for three selections from *Leaves of Grass* by Walt Whitman, copyright 1924 by Doubleday and Company, Inc.

E. P. DUTTON AND COMPANY, INC., for "The Little Lost Pup" from *Death and General Putnam* by Arthur Guiterman, copyright 1935 by E. P. Dutton and Company, Inc.

FARRAR, STRAUS AND COMPANY, INC., for "Atlantic Charter" from *The Island* by Francis Brett Young.

MRS. CHARLOTTE PERKINS STETSON GILMAN for "Similar Cases" from *In This Our World*.

MRS. ARTHUR GUITERMAN for "Under the Goal Posts" by Arthur Guiterman.

HARCOURT BRACE AND COMPANY, INC., for lines from "The People, Yes" by Carl Sandburg from the volume of the same name, copyright 1936 by Harcourt, Brace and Co.

HARPER AND BROTHERS for "Simon the Cyrenian Speaks" from *Color* by Countee Cullen, copyright 1925 by Harper and Brothers; and for "Flash" from *City Ballads* by Will Carleton.

HENRY HOLT AND COMPANY, INC., for "The Listeners" from *Collected Poems* by Walter de la Mare; "The Runaway" from *Complete Poems of Robert Frost,* copyright 1930, 1939 by Henry Holt and Company; "Grass" from *Corn Huskers* by Carl Sandburg, copyright 1918 by Henry Holt and Company; "When I Was One and Twenty" from *A Shropshire Lad* by A. E. Housman.

HOUGHTON MIFFLIN COMPANY for "The Enchanted Shirt" and "Jim Bludso" from *Poems* by John Hay; "Pandora's Song" from *Poems and Poetic Dramas* by William Vaughan Moody; "Opportunity" from *Poems* by Edward Rowland Sill; "Bedouin Love Song" and "Storm Song" from *Bayard Taylor's Poems;* selections from *The Complete Poems of Ralph Waldo Emerson, The Complete Poems of Oliver Wendell Holmes, The Complete Poems of Henry Wadsworth Longfellow, The Complete Poems of John Greenleaf Whittier, The Complete Poems of James Russell Lowell* and *The Complete Poems of Robert Browning.*

J. B. LIPPINCOTT COMPANY for "Sheridan's Ride" from *Poetical Works* by T. B. Read; "A Song of Sherwood," "Forty Singing Seamen" and "The Highwayman," copyright 1906, 1934 by Alfred Noyes, from *Collected Poems in One Volume* by Alfred Noyes, and "The Admiral's Ghost," copyright 1913, 1941 by Alfred Noyes from the same volume; "Prayer for a Pilot" from *Poems* by Cecil Roberts; "Peg-leg's Fiddle" and "The Ballad of the *Ivanhoe*" from *Fenceless Meadows* by Bill Adams; L. LAMPREY for "Lincoln" from *Days of the Leaders*.

LITTLE BROWN AND COMPANY for "I'm Nobody! Who Are You?", "I Never Saw a Moor," "There Is No Frigate" and "Precious Words" from *Poems by Emily Dickinson* edited by Martha Dickinson Bianchi; "Fate" by S. M. Spaulding.

[v]

Acknowledgments

LOTHROP, LEE AND SHEPARD COMPANY, INC., for "The Coming American" by Sam Walter Foss.

THE MACMILLAN COMPANY for "The Broncho That Would Not Be Broken" from *The Chinese Nightingale and Other Poems* by Vachel Lindsay, copyright 1917, 1945; lines from "Dauber" from *The Story of a Roundhouse* by John Masefield, copyright 1912 by the Macmillan Company.

SISTER M. MADELEVA for "Beech Trees."

VIRGIL MARKHAM for "Brotherhood" by Edwin Markham.

JUANITA J. MILLER for "Columbus" and lines from "To Byron" from *Complete Poems of Joaquin Miller*.

DAVID MORTON for "Old Ships."

NEW YORK HERALD TRIBUNE for "High Flight" by John Gillespie Magee, Jr., copyright February 8, 1942.

OXFORD UNIVERSITY PRESS for "God's Grandeur" from *Poems by Gerard Manley Hopkins*.

MESSRS. G. P. PUTNAM'S SONS for "In Flanders Fields" from *In Flanders Fields and Other Poems* by John McCrae; "Each in His Own Tongue" from *Each in His Own Tongue and Other Poems* by W. H. Carruth.

RANDOM HOUSE, INC., for "The Express" copyright, 1942, by Stephen Spender, and "Ultima Ratio Regum" by Stephen Spender, from *Poems* by Stephen Spender, © 1934 by Modern Library Inc.

CHARLES SCRIBNER'S SONS for lines from "The Marshes of Glynn" from *Poems* by Sidney Lanier; "The Celestial Surgeon," "Requiem," "The Vagabond" and "Christmas at Sea" from *Collected Poems* by Robert Louis Stevenson, and "Camper's Night Song" from *Travels with a Donkey* by Robert Louis Stevenson; "Four Things" from *The Toiling of Felix* by Henry Van Dyke; "I Have a Rendezvous with Death" from *Poems* by Alan Seeger.

THE VIKING PRESS, INC., for "Snake" from *Collected Poems* by D. H. Lawrence, copyright 1929 by Jonathan Cape and Harrison Smith, Inc.

Dedicated

To

THEODORE HERBERT TAYLOR
who was a boy when this book was first made

and to his son

MALCOLM HERBERT TAYLOR

COMPILER'S FOREWORD

I like to think that this anthology has been used and liked by American boys for twenty-eight years and that I can now dedicate the revised edition to the son of the boy for whom it was first made.

In adding more than forty new poems by poets of our own day, in place of some of the older poems, I have been guided by a number of boys who loved the old book but liked the idea of bringing the collection up-to-date. I am grateful for advice, to them and to several older poetry lovers who know a good deal about boys' tastes.

Many of the poems in this book belong to the great poetry of the centuries; other verses, though not great, are here because they are worthy of your liking and touch upon the varied experiences of modern boys and young men. It's all here together for you to sample and enjoy, according to your temperament or mood. In youth the appetite for all new things in experience and art is fresh and experimental. You have a right to like anything that seems to you true or interesting or challenging: from any point of view. No one boy will like all the poems, nor do I wish it to be so. I intend this as a companionable volume to help you find what pleases you. Then you can follow to their own volumes the poets you like best.

I have tried to represent many of the newer poets who have said something clearly or beautifully—or both—for boys, in new verse forms, new thinking, the new spirit of our times. As you grow, in experience of life and acquaintance with poetry, you will easily sort out the greater from the lesser of these.

Occasionally the boys who read and studied this book in manuscript noted that a poem was "difficult" or "failed to get through." Sometimes, on my own restudy of the poem, I granted the objection and discarded the poem, but often I left it in, confident that it would require only rereading to make it not only understandable but likable. Many interesting expressions of art, including some great and enduring works, are not completely clear, even to adults, at first impression. And I have put in one poem which seemed to me cruel, because I found that boys understand it and like it.

I salute again Franklin K. Mathiews, that great Scout beloved by men and boys our country over, and I quote from the Foreword he wrote twenty-eight years ago for the first edition of this book—words as true today as they were then: "If inventors, through products of their genius are able to make life easier and more comfortable, with the same insight of genius poets serve us equally well in making us more conscious of the wonder and beauty of our world."

Helen Dean Fish

CONTENTS

Part One

STORY POEMS

There is no frigate like a book
To take us lands away,
Nor any coursers like a page
Of prancing poetry.
This traverse may the poorest take
Without oppress of toll,
How frugal is the chariot
That bears a human soul!

Emily Dickinson

BALLAD OF EAST AND WEST

RUDYARD KIPLING

O*h, East is East, and West is West, and never the twain
shall meet,*
*Till Earth and Sky stand presently at God's great Judgment
Seat;*
*But there is neither East nor West, Border, nor Breed, nor
Birth,*
*When two strong men stand face to face, tho' they come from
the ends of the earth!*

Kamal is out with twenty men to raise the Borderside,
And he has lifted the Colonel's mare that is the Colonel's
pride;
He has lifted her out of the stable-door between the dawn
and the day,
And turned the calkins upon her feet, and ridden her far
away.
Then up and spoke the Colonel's son that led a troop of the
Guides:
"Is there never a man of all my men can say where Kamal
hides?"

Then up and spoke Mahommed Khan, the son of the Res-
saldar:
"If ye know the track of the morning-mist, ye know where
his pickets are.
At dusk he harries the Abazai—at dawn he is into Bonair,
But he must go by Fort Bukloh to his own place to fare,
So if ye gallop to Fort Bukloh as fast as a bird can fly,

By the favour of God ye may cut him off ere he win to the
    Tongue of Jagai.
But if he be past the Tongue of Jagai, right swiftly turn ye
    then,
For the length and the breadth of that grisly plain is sown
    with Kamal's men.
There is rock to the left, and rock to the right, and low lean
    thorn between,
And ye may hear a breech-bolt snick where never a man is
    seen."

The Colonel's son has taken a horse, and a raw rough dun
    was he,
With the mouth of a bell and the heart of Hell and the head
    of a gallows-tree.
The Colonel's son to the Fort has won, they bid him stay to
    eat—
Who rides at the tail of a Border thief, he sits not long at
    his meat.
He's up and away from Fort Bukloh as fast as he can fly,
Till he was aware of his father's mare in the gut of the
    Tongue of Jagai,
Till he was aware of his father's mare with Kamal upon her
    back,
And when he could spy the white of her eye, he made the
    pistol crack.
He has fired once, he has fired twice, but the whistling ball
    went wide.
"Ye shoot like a soldier," Kamal said. "Show now if ye can
    ride."

It's up and over the Tongue of Jagai, as blown dust-devils go,
The dun he fled like a stag of ten, but the mare like a barren
    doe.
The dun he leaned against the bit and slugged his head above,

[4]

But the red mare played with the snaffle-bars, as a maiden
plays with a glove.
There was rock to the left, and rock to the right, and low
lean thorn between,
And thrice he heard a breech-bolt snick tho' never a man was
seen.
They have ridden the low moon out of the sky, their hoofs
drum up the dawn,
The dun he went like a wounded bull, but the mare like a
new-roused fawn.
The dun he fell at a water-course—in a woeful heap fell he,
And Kamal has turned the red mare back, and pulled the
rider free.
He has knocked the pistol out of his hand—small room was
there to strive,
" 'Twas only by favour of mine," quoth he, "ye rode so long
alive:
There was not a rock for twenty mile, there was not a clump
of tree,
But covered a man of my own men with his rifle cocked on
his knee.
If I had raised my bridle-hand, as I have held it low,
The little jackals that flee so fast were feasting all in a row:
If I had bowed my head on my breast, as I have held it high,
The kite that whistles above us now were gorged till she
could not fly."

Lightly answered the Colonel's son: "Do good to bird and
beast,
But count who come for the broken meats before thou makest
a feast.
If there should follow a thousand swords to carry my bones
away,
Belike the price of a jackal's meal were more than a thief
could pay.

They will feed their horse on the standing crop, their men on
    the garnered grain,
The thatch of the byres will serve their fires when all the
    cattle are slain.
But if thou thinkest the price be fair,—thy brethren wait to
    sup,
The hound is kin to the jackal-spawn,—howl, dog, and call
    them up!
And if thou thinkest the price be high, in steer and gear and
    stack,
Give me my father's mare again, and I'll fight my own way
    back!"

Kamal has gripped him by the hand and set him upon his
    feet.
"No talk shall be of dogs," said he, "when wolf and grey
    wolf meet.
May I eat dirt if thou hast hurt of me in deed or breath;
What dam of lances brought thee forth to jest at the dawn
    with Death?"
Lightly answered the Colonel's son: "I hold by the blood of
    my clan:
Take up the mare for my father's gift—by God, she has
    carried a man!"
The red mare ran to the Colonel's son, and nuzzled against
    his breast;
"We be two strong men," said Kamal then, "but she loveth
    the younger best.
So she shall go with a lifter's dower, my turquoise studded
    rein,
My broidered saddle and saddle-cloth, and silver stirrups
    twain."
The Colonel's son a pistol drew and held it muzzle-end,
"Ye have taken the one from a foe," said he; "will ye take
    the mate from a friend?"

"A gift for a gift," said Kamal straight; "a limb for the risk
of a limb.
Thy father has sent his son to me, I'll send my son to him!"

With that he whistled his only son, that dropped from a
mountain-crest—
He trod the ling like a buck in spring, and he looked like a
lance in rest.
"Now here is thy master," Kamal said, "who leads a troop of
the Guides,
And thou must ride at his left side as shield on shoulder rides.
Till Death or I cut loose the tie, at camp and board and
bed,
Thy life is his—thy fate it is to guard him with thy head.
So, thou must eat the White Queen's meat, and all her foes
are thine,
And thou must harry thy father's hold for the peace of the
Border-line,
And thou must make a trooper tough and hack thy way to
power—
Belike they will raise thee to Ressaldar when I am hanged in
Peshawur."

They have looked each other between the eyes, and there
they found no fault,
They have taken the Oath of the Brother-in-Blood, on
leavened bread and salt:
They have taken the Oath of the Brother-in-Blood on fire
and fresh-cut sod,
On the hilt and the haft of the Khyber knife, and the Won-
drous Names of God.
The Colonel's son he rides the mare, and Kamal's boy the
dun,
And two have come back to Fort Bukloh where there went
forth but one.

[7]

And when they drew to the Quarter-Guard, full **twenty**
    swords flew clear—
There was not a man but carried his feud with the blood of
    the mountaineer.
"Ha' done! ha' done!" said the Colonel's son. "Put up **the**
    steel at your sides!
Last night ye had struck at a Border thief—tonight 'tis **a**
    man of the Guides!"

Oh, East is East, and West is West, and never the twain
    shall meet,
Till Earth and Sky stand presently at God's great Judgment
    Seat;
But there is neither East nor West, Border, nor Breed, nor
    Birth,
When two strong men stand face to face, tho' they come from
    the ends of the earth!

*Rudyard Kipling was born and brought up in India, and at eighteen
started to work on a newspaper in Lahore. His journalistic work led him
to live, for a time, in a British army post, and it was there that he became
acquainted with the British soldier, "Tommy Atkins," and many of the
characters who appeared later in his "Barrack Room Ballads."*

GUNGA DIN

RUDYARD KIPLING

You may talk o' gin and beer
When you're quartered safe out 'ere,
An' you're sent to penny-fights an' Aldershot it;
But when it comes to slaughter
You will do your work on water,
An' you'll lick the bloomin' boots of 'im that's got it.
Now in Injia's sunny clime,

Where I used to spend my time
A-servin' of 'Er Majesty the Queen,
Of all them blackfaced crew
The finest man I knew
Was our regimental bhisti, Gunga Din.
    He was "Din! Din! Din!
  You limpin' lump o' brick-dust, Gunga Din!
    Hi! slippery *hitherao!*
    Water, get it! *Panee lao!* [1]
  You squidgy-nosed old idol, Gunga Din!"

The uniform 'e wore
Was nothin' much before,
An' rather less than 'arf o' that be'ind,
For a piece o' twisty rag
An' a goatskin water-bag
Was all the field equipment 'e could find.
When the sweatin' troop-train lay
In a sidin' through the day,
Where the 'eat would make your bloomin' eyebrows
    crawl,
We shouted "Harry By!" [2]
Till our throats were bricky-dry,
Then we wopped 'im 'cause 'e couldn't serve us all.
    It was "Din! Din! Din!
  You 'eathen, where the mischief 'ave you been?
    You put some *juldee* [3] in it
    Or I'll *marrow* [4] you this minute
  If you don't fill up my helmet, Gunga Din!"

'E would dot an' carry one
Till the longest day was done;
An' 'e didn't seem to know the use o' fear.
If we charged or broke or cut,

[1] Bring water swiftly.   [2] Mr. Atkins' equivalent for "O Brother."
[3] Be quick.   [4] Hit you.

You could bet your bloomin' nut,
'E'd be waitin' fifty paces right flank rear.
With 'is *mussick* [5] on 'is back,
'E would skip with our attack,
An' watch us till the bugles made "Retire"
An' for all 'is dirty 'ide
'E was white, clear white, inside
When 'e went to tend the wounded under fire!
    It was "Din! Din! Din!"
  With the bullets kickin' dust spots on the green
    When the cartridges ran out,
    You could hear the front-ranks shout,
  "Hi! ammunition-mules an' Gunga Din!"

I shan't forgit the night
When I dropped be'ind the fight
With a bullet where my belt-plate should 'a' been.
I was chokin' mad with thirst,
An' the man that spied me first
Was our good old grinnin', gruntin' Gunga Din.
'E lifted up my 'ead,
An' 'e plugged me where I bled,
An' 'e gave me 'arf-a-pint o' water-green:
It was crawlin' an' it stunk,
But of all the drinks I've drunk,
I'm gratefullest to one from Gunga Din.
    It was "Din! Din! Din!
  'Ere's a beggar with a bullet through 'is spleen;
    'E's chawin' up the ground,
  An' 'e's kickin' all around:
  For Gawd's sake git the water, Gunga Din!"

'E carried me away
To where a dooli lay,
  An' a bullet come an' drilled the beggar clean—

[5] Water-skin.

'E put me safe inside,
An' just before 'e died,
"I 'ope you liked your drink," sez Gunga Din.
So I'll meet 'im later on
At the place where 'e is gone—
Where it's always double drill and no canteen;
'E'll be squattin' on the coals
Givin' drink to poor damned souls,
An' I'll get a swig in hell from Gunga Din!
    Yes, Din! Din! Din!
  You Lazarushian-leather Gunga Din!
    Though I've belted you and flayed you,
    By the livin' Gawd that made you,
  You're a better man than I am, Gunga Din!

HE FELL AMONG THIEVES

HENRY NEWBOLT

Henry John Newbolt may have inherited his love of the sea from a celebrated grandfather of His Majesty's Navy in the early 19th century. He began writing verse when he was sixteen, and continued during his career as a barrister. He became Professor of Poetry at Oxford University in 1911 and died in 1938.

Ye have robbed," said he, "ye have slaughtered and made
    an end,
  Take your ill-got plunder and bury the dead;
What will ye more of your guest and sometime friend?"
  "Blood for our blood," they said.

He laughed: "If one may settle the score for five,
  I am ready; but let the reckoning stand till day:
I have loved the sunlight as dearly as any alive."
  "You shall die at dawn," said they.

He Fell Among Thieves

He flung his empty revolver down the slope,
  He climbed alone to the Eastward edge of the trees.
All night long in a dream untroubled of hope
  He brooded, clasping his knees.

He did not hear the monotonous roar that fills
  The ravine where the Yassin river sullenly flows:
He did not see the starlight on the Laspur hills,
  Or the far Afghan snows.

He saw the April noon on his books aglow,
  The wistaria trailing in at the window wide;
He heard his father's voice from the terrace below
  Calling him down to ride.

He saw the gray little church across the park,
  The mounds that hide the loved and honored dead;
The Norman arch, the chancel softly dark,
  The brasses black and red.

He saw the School Close, sunny and green,
  The runner beside him, the stand by the parapet wall,
The distant tape and the crowd roaring between,
  His own name over all.

He saw the dark wainscot and the timbered roof,
  The long tables and the faces merry and keen;
The College Eight and their trainer dining aloof,
  The Dons on the dais serene.

He watched the liner's stem ploughing the foam,
  He felt her trembling speed and the thrash of her screw;
He heard her passengers' voices talking of home,
  He saw the flag she flew.

And now it was dawn. He rose strong on his feet,
   And strode to his ruined camp below the wood;
He drank the breath of the morning cool and sweet;
   His murderers round him stood.

Light on the Laspur hills was broadening fast,
   The blood-red snow-peaks chilled to a dazzling white;
He turned and saw the golden circle at last,
   Cut by the Eastern height.

"O glorious Life, Who dwellest in earth and sun,
   I have lived, I praise and adore Thee."
                    A sword swept.
Over the pass the voices one by one
   Faded, and the hill slept.

THE RED THREAD OF HONOR

FRANCIS HASTINGS DOYLE

Eleven men of England
   A breast-work charged in vain:
Eleven men of England
   Lie stripp'd, and gash'd, and slain.
Slain; but of foes that guarded
   Their rock-built fortress well,
Some twenty had been master'd,
   When the last soldier fell.

The robber-chief mused deeply,
   Above those daring dead;
"Bring here," at length he shouted,
   "Bring quick, the battle thread.

[13]

Let Eblis blast for ever
    Their souls, if Allah will;
But *we* must keep unbroken
    The old rules of the Hill.

"Before the Ghiznee tiger
    Leapt forth to burn and slay;
Before the holy Prophet
    Taught our grim tribes to pray;
Before Secunder's lances
    Pierced through each Indian glen;
The mountain laws of honor
    Were framed for fearless men.

"Still, when a chief dies bravely,
    We bind with green one wrist—
Green for the brave, for heroes
    One crimson thread we twist.
Say ye, oh gallant Hillman,
    For these, whose life has fled,
Which is the fitting color,
    The green one, or the red?"

"Our brethren, laid in honor'd graves, may wear
    Their green reward," each noble savage said;
"To these, whom hawks and hungry wolves shall **tear**,
    Who dares deny the red?"

Thus conquering hate, and stedfast to the right,
    Fresh from the heart that haughty verdict came;
Beneath a waning moon, each spectral height
    Roll'd back its loud acclaim.

Once more the chief gazed keenly
    Down on those daring dead;

From his good sword their heart's blood
    Crept to that crimson thread.

Once more he cried, "The judgment,
    Good friends, is wise and true,
But though the red be given,
    Have we not more to do?

"These were not stirr'd by anger,
    Nor yet by lust made bold;
Renown they thought above them,
    Nor did they look for gold.
To them their leader's signal
    Was as the voice of God:
Unmoved, and uncomplaining,
    The path it show'd they trod.

"As, without sound or struggle,
    The stars unhurrying march,
Where Allah's finger guides them,
    Through yonder purple arch,
These Franks, sublimely silent,
    Without a quicken'd breath,
Went, in the strength of duty,
    Straight to their goal of death.

"If I were now to ask you,
    To name our bravest man,
Ye all at once would answer,
    They call'd him Mehrab Khan.
He sleeps among his fathers,
    Dear to our native land,
With the bright mark he bled for
    Firm round his faithful hand.

"The songs they sing of Roostum
　　Fill all the past with light;
If truth be in their music,
　　He was a noble knight.
But were those heroes living,
　　And strong for battle still,
Would Mehrab Khan or Roostum
　　Have climb'd, like these, the Hill?"

And they replied, "Though Mehrab Khan was brave,
　　As chief, he chose himself what risks to run;
Prince Roostum lied, his forfeit life to save,
　　Which these had never done."

"Enough!" he shouted fiercely;
　　"Doom'd though they be to hell,
Bind fast the crimson trophy
　　Round *both* wrists—bind it well.
Who knows but that great Allah
　　May grudge such matchless men,
With none so deck'd in heaven,
　　To the fiend's flaming den?"

Then all those gallant robbers
　　Shouted a stern "Amen!"
They raised the slaughter'd sergeant,
　　They raised his mangled ten.
And when we found their bodies
　　Left bleaching in the wind,
Around both wrists in glory
　　That crimson thread was twined.

YUSSOUF

JAMES RUSSELL LOWELL

A stranger came one night to Yussouf's tent,
Saying, "Behold one outcast and in dread,
Against whose life the blow of power is bent,
Who flies, and hath not where to lay his head;
I come to thee for shelter and for food,
To Yussouf, called through all our tribes 'The Good.' "

"This tent is mine," said Yussouf, "but no more
Than it is God's; come in, and be at peace;
Freely shalt thou partake of all my store
As I of his who buildeth over these
Our tents his glorious roof of night and day,
And at whose door none ever yet heard Nay."

So Yussouf entertained his guest that night,
And, waking him ere day, said: "Here is gold,
My swiftest horse is saddled for thy flight,
Depart before the prying day grow bold."
As one lamp lights another, nor grows less,
So nobleness enkindleth nobleness.

That inward light the stranger's face made grand,
Which shines from all self-conquest; kneeling low,
He bowed his forehead upon Yussouf's hand,
Sobbing: "O Sheik, I cannot leave thee so;
I will repay thee; all this thou hast done
Unto that Ibrahim who slew thy son!"

"Take thrice the gold," said Yussouf, "for with thee
Into the desert, never to return,
My one black thought shall ride away from me;
First-born, for whom by day and night I yearn,
Balanced and just are all of God's decrees;
Thou art avenged, my first-born, sleep in peace!"

THE HIGHWAYMAN

ALFRED NOYES

PART ONE

The wind was a torrent of darkness among the gusty trees,
The moon was a ghostly galleon tossed upon cloudy seas,
The road was a ribbon of moonlight over the purple moor,
And the highwayman came riding—
      Riding—riding—
The highwayman came riding, up to the old inn-door.

He'd a French cocked-hat on his forehead, a bunch of lace
    at his chin,
A coat of the claret velvet, and breeches of brown doe-skin;
They fitted with never a wrinkle: his boots were up to the
    thigh!
And he rode with a jewelled twinkle,
      His pistol butts a-twinkle,
His rapier hilt a-twinkle, under the jewelled sky.

Over the cobbles he clattered and clashed in the dark inn-
    yard,
And he tapped with his whip on the shutters, but all was
    locked and barred;
He whistled a tune to the window, and who should be wait-
    ing there
But the landlord's black-eyed daughter,
      Bess, the landlord's daughter,
Plaiting a dark red love-knot into her long black hair.

And dark in the dark old inn-yard a stable-wicket creaked
Where Tim the ostler listened; his face was white and
    peaked;

His eyes were hollows of madness, his hair like mouldy hay,
But he loved the landlord's daughter,
      The landlord's red-lipped daughter,
Dumb as a dog he listened, and he heard the robber say—

"One kiss, my bonny sweetheart, I'm after a prize to-night,
But I shall be back with the yellow gold before the morning
    light;
Yet, if they press me sharply, and harry me through the day,
Then look for me by moonlight,
      Watch for me by moonlight,
I'll come to thee by moonlight, though hell should bar the
    way."

He rose upright in the stirrups; he scarce could reach her
    hand,
But she loosened her hair i' the casement! His face burnt like
    a brand
As the black cascade of perfume came tumbling over his
    breast;
And he kissed its waves in the moonlight,
      (Oh, sweet black waves in the
        moonlight!)
Then he tugged at his rein in the moonlight, and galloped
    away to the West.

PART TWO

He did not come in the dawning; he did not come at noon;
And out o' the tawny sunset, before the rise o' the moon,
When the road was a gipsy's ribbon, looping the purple
    moor,
A red-coat troop came marching—
      Marching—marching—
King George's men came marching, up to the old inn-door.

The Highwayman

They said no word to the landlord, they drank his ale instead,
But they gagged his daughter and bound her to the foot of
  her narrow bed;
Two of them knelt at her casement, with muskets at their
  side!
There was death at every window;
  And hell at one dark window;
For Bess could see, through her casement, the road that he
  would ride.

They had tied her up to attention, with many a sniggering
  jest;
They had bound a musket beside her, with the barrel be-
  neath her breast!
"Now keep good watch!" and they kissed her.
  She heard the dead man say—
Look for me by moonlight;
  Watch for me by moonlight;
I'll come to thee by moonlight, though hell should bar the
  way!

She twisted her hands behind her; but all the knots held
  good!
She writhed her hands till her fingers were wet with sweat
  or blood!
They stretched and strained in the darkness, and the hours
  crawled by like years,
Till, now, on the stroke of midnight,
  Cold, on the stroke of midnight,
The tip of one finger touched it! The trigger at least was
  hers!

The tip of one finger touched it; she strove no more for the
  rest!
Up, she stood up to attention, with the barrel beneath her
  breast,

She would not risk their hearing; she would not strive again;
For the road lay bare in the moonlight;
            Black and bare in the moonlight;
And the blood of her veins in the moonlight throbbed to her
    love's refrain.

Tlot-tlot; tlot-tlot! Had they heard it? The horse-hoofs ring-
    ing clear;
Tlot-tlot, tlot-tlot, in the distance? Were they deaf that they
    did not hear?
Down the ribbon of moonlight, over the brow of the hill,
The highwayman came riding,
            Riding, riding!
The red-coats looked to their priming! She stood up, straight
    and still!

Tlot-tlot, in the frosty silence! *Tlot-tlot,* in the echoing
    night!
Nearer he came and nearer! Her face was like a light!
Her eyes grew wide for a moment; she drew one last deep
    breath,
Then her finger moved in the moonlight,
            Her musket shattered the moonlight,
Shattered her breast in the moonlight and warned him—with
    her death.

He turned; he spurred to the West; he did not know who
    stood
Bowed, with her head o'er the musket, drenched with her
    own red blood!
Not till the dawn he heard it, his face grew grey to hear
How Bess, the landlord's daughter,
            The landlord's black-eyed daughter,
Had watched for her love in the moonlight, and died in the
    darkness there.

Back, he spurred like a madman, shrieking a curse to the sky,
With the white road smoking behind him and his rapier
brandished high!
Blood-red were his spurs i' the golden noon; wine-red was
his velvet coat,
When they shot him down on the highway,
Down like a dog on the highway,
And he lay in his blood on the highway, with a bunch of lace
at his throat.

And still of a winter's night, they say, when the wind is in
the trees,
When the moon is a ghostly galleon tossed upon cloudy seas,
When the road is a ribbon of moonlight over the purple
moor,
A highwayman comes riding—
Riding—riding—
A highwayman comes riding, up to the old inn-door.

Over the cobbles he clatters and clangs in the dark inn-yard;
He taps with his whip on the shutter, but all is locked and
barred;
He whistles a tune to the window, and who should be waiting
there
But the landlord's black-eyed daughter,
Bess, the landlord's daughter,
Plaiting a dark red love-knot into her long black hair.

JESSE JAMES

(A Design in Red and Yellow for a Nickel Library)

WILLIAM ROSE BENÉT

Jesse James was a two-gun man,
   (Roll on, Missouri!)
Strong-arm chief of an outlaw clan.
   (From Kansas to Illinois!)
He twirled an old Colt forty-five;
   (Roll on, Missouri!)
They never took Jesse James alive.
   (Roll, Missouri, roll!)

Jesse James was King of the Wes';
   (Cataracks in the Missouri!)
He'd a di'mon' heart in his lef' breas';
   (Brown Missouri rolls!)
He'd a fire in his heart no hurt could stifle;
   (Thunder, Missouri!)
Lion eyes an' a Winchester rifle.
   (Missouri, roll down!)

Jesse James rode a pinto hawse;
Come at night to a water-cawse;
Tetched with the rowel that pinto's flank;
She sprung the torrent from bank to bank.

Jesse rode through a sleepin' town;
Looked the moonlit street both up an' down;
Crack-crack-crack, the street ran flames
An' a great voice cried, "I'm Jesse James!"

Hawse an' afoot they're after Jess!
   (Roll on, Missouri!)

[23]

Spurrin' an' spurrin'—but he's gone Wes'.
  (*Brown Missouri rolls!*)
He was ten foot tall when he stood in his boots;
    (*Lightnin' light the Missouri!*)
More'n a match fer sich galoots.
    (*Roll, Missouri, roll!*)

Jesse James rode outa the sage;
Roun' the rocks come the swayin' stage;
Straddlin' the road a giant stan's
An' a great voice bellers, "Throw up yer han's!"

Jesse raked in the di'mon' rings,
The big gold watches an' the yuther things;
Jesse divvied 'em then an' thar
With a cryin' child had lost her mar.

The U.S. troopers is after Jess;
    (*Roll on, Missouri!*)
Their hawses sweat foam, but he's gone Wes';
    (*Hear Missouri roar!*)
He was broad as a b'ar, he'd a ches' like a drum,
    (*Wind an' rain through Missouri!*)
An' his red hair flamed like Kingdom Come.
    (*Missouri down to the sea!*)

Jesse James all alone in the rain
Stopped an' stuck up the Eas'-boun' train;
Swayed through the coaches with horns an' a tail,
Lit out with the bullion an' the registered mail.

Jess made 'em all turn green with fright
Quakin' in the aisles in the pitch-black night;
An' he give all the bullion to a pore ole tramp
Campin' nigh the cuttin' in the dirt an' damp.

The whole U.S. is after Jess;
    (*Roll on, Missouri!*)
The son-of-a-gun, if he ain't gone Wes';
    (*Missouri to the sea!*)
He could chaw cold iron an' spit blue flame;
    (*Cataracks down the Missouri!*)
He rode on a catamount he'd larned to tame.
    (*Hear that Missouri roll!*)

Jesse James rode into a bank;
Give his pinto a tetch on the flank;
Jumped the teller's window with an awful crash;
Heaved up the safe an' twirled his mustache;

He said, "So long, boys!" He yelped, "So long!
Feelin' porely today—I ain't feelin' strong!"
Rode right through the wall a-goin' crack-crack-crack—
Took the safe home to mother in a gunny-sack.

They're creepin', they're crawlin', they're stalkin' Jess;
    (*Roll on, Missouri!*)
They's a rumor he's gone much further Wes';
    (*Roll, Missouri, roll!*)
They's word of a cayuse hitched to the bars
    (*Ruddy clouds on Missouri!*)
Of a golden sunset that busts into stars.
    (*Missouri, roll down!*)

Jesse James rode hell fer leather;
He was a hawse an' a man together;
In a cave in a mountain high up in air
He lived with a rattlesnake, a wolf, an' a bear.

Jesse's heart was as sof' as a woman;
Fer guts an' stren'th he was sooper-human;

Jesse James

He could put six shots through a woodpecker's eye
And take in one swaller a gallon o' rye.

They sought him here an' they sought him there,
    (Roll on, Missouri!)
But he strides by night through the ways of the air;
    (Brown Missouri rolls!)
They say he was took an' they say he is dead,
    (Thunder, Missouri!)
But he ain't—he's a sunset overhead!
    (Missouri down to the sea!)

Jesse James was a Hercules.
When he went through the woods he tore up the trees.
When he went on the plains he smoked the groun'
An' the hull lan' shuddered fer miles aroun'.

Jesse James wore a red bandanner
That waved on the breeze like the Star Spangled Banner;
In seven states he cut up dadoes.
He's gone with the buffler an' the desperadoes.

Yes, Jesse James was a two-gun man
    (Roll on, Missouri!)
The same as when this song began;
    (From Kansas to Illinois!)
An' when you see a sunset bust into flames
    (Lightnin' light the Missouri!)
Or a thunderstorm blaze—thar's Jesse James!
    (Hear that Missouri roll!)

THE ADMIRAL'S GHOST

ALFRED NOYES

I tell you a tale to-night
  Which a seaman told to me,
With eyes that gleamed in the lanthorn light
  And a voice as low as the sea.

You could almost hear the stars
  Twinkling up in the sky,
And the old wind woke and moaned in the spars,
  And the same old waves went by,

Singing the same old song
  As ages and ages ago,
While he froze my blood in that deep-sea night
  With the things that he seemed to know.

A bare foot pattered on deck;
  Ropes creaked; then—all grew still,
And he pointed his finger straight in my face
  And growled, as a sea-dog will.

"Do 'ee know who Nelson was?
  That pore little shrivelled form
With the patch on his eye and the pinned-up sleeve
  And a soul like a North Sea storm?

"Ask of the Devonshire men!
  They know, and they'll tell you true;
He wasn't the pore little chawed-up chap
  That Hardy thought he knew.

"He wasn't the man you think!
    His patch was a dern disguise!
For he knew that they'd find him out, d'you see,
    If they looked him in both his eyes.

"He was twice as big as he seemed;
    But his clothes were cunningly made.
He'd both of his hairy arms all right!
    The sleeve was a trick of the trade.

"You've heard of sperrits, no doubt;
    Well, there's more in the matter than that!
But he wasn't the patch and he wasn't the sleeve,
    And he wasn't the laced cocked-hat.

"*Nelson was just—a Ghost!*
    You may laugh! But the Devonshire men
They knew that he'd come when England called,
    And they know that he'll come again.

"I'll tell you the way it was
    (For none of the landsmen know),
And to tell it you right, you must go a-starn
    Two hundred years or so.

"The waves were lapping and slapping
    The same as they are to-day;
And Drake lay dying aboard his ship
    In Nombre Dios Bay.

"The scent of the foreign flowers
    Came floating all around;
'But I'd give my soul for the smell o' the pitch,'
    Says he, 'in Plymouth sound.

[28]

" 'What shall I do,' he says,
 'When the guns begin to roar,
An' England wants me, and me not there
 To shatter 'er foes once more?'

"(You've heard what he said, maybe,
 But I'll mark you the p'ints again;
For I want you to box your compass right
 And get my story plain.)

" 'You must take my drum,' he says,
 'To the old sea-wall at home;
And if ever you strike that drum,' he says,
 'Why, strike me blind, I'll come!

" 'If England needs me, dead
 Or living, I'll rise that day!
I'll rise from the darkness under the sea
 Ten thousand miles away.'

"That's what he said; and he died;
 An' his pirates, listenin' roun'
With their crimson doublets and jewelled swords
 That flashed as the sun went down.

"They sewed him up in his shroud
 With a round-shot top and toe,
To sink him under the salt sharp sea
 Where all good seamen go.

"They lowered him down in the deep,
 And there in the sunset light
They boomed a broadside over his grave,
 As meanin' to say 'Good-night.'

[29]

"They sailed away in the dark
    To the dear little isle they knew;
And they hung his drum by the old sea-wall
    The same as he told them to.

"Two hundred years went by,
    And the guns began to roar,
And England was fighting hard for her life,
    As ever she fought of yore.

" 'It's only my dead that count,'
    She said, as she says to-day;
'It isn't the ships and it isn't the guns
    'Ull sweep Trafalgar's Bay.'

"D'you guess who Nelson was?
    You may laugh, but it's true as true!
There was more in that pore little chawed-up chap
    Than ever his best friend knew.

"The foe was creepin' close,
    In the dark, to our white-cliffed isle;
They were ready to leap at England's throat,
    When—O, you may smile, you may smile;

"But—ask of the Devonshire men;
    For they heard in the dead of night
The roll of a drum, and they saw him pass
    On a ship all shining white.

"He stretched out his dead cold face
    And he sailed in the grand old way!
The fishes had taken an eye and his arm,
    But he swept Trafalgar's Bay.

"Nelson—was Francis Drake!
  O, what matters the uniform,
Or the patch on your eye or your pinned-up sleeve,
  If your soul's like a North Sea storm?"

*The English poet, Alfred Noyes, has written some of the finest ballads
of modern times. "The Admiral's Ghost" is based on an old Devon-
shire legend. Trafalgar was Nelson's greatest naval victory and the
battle in which he lost his life. It broke Napoleon's naval power forever.*

FORTY SINGING SEAMEN

ALFRED NOYES

Across the seas of Wonderland to Mogadore we plodded,
Forty singing seamen in an old black barque,
And we landed in the twilight where a Polyphemus nodded,
With his battered moon-eye winking red and yellow through
    the dark!
  For his eye was growing mellow,
  Rich and ripe and red and yellow,
As was time, since old Ulysses made him bellow in the dark!
Since Ulysses bunged his eye up with a pine-torch in the dark!

Were they mountains in the gloaming or the giant's ugly
    shoulders
Just beneath the rolling eye-ball, with its bleared and vinous
    glow,
Red and yellow o'er the purple of the pines among the
    boulders
And the shaggy horror brooding on the sullen slopes below,
Were they pines among the boulders
  Or the hair upon his shoulders?

We were only simple seamen, so of course we didn't know.
We were simple singing seamen, so of course we couldn't
know.

But we crossed a plain of poppies, and we came upon a foun-
tain
Not of water, but of jewels, like a spray of leaping fire;
And behind it, in an emerald glade, beneath a golden moun-
tain
There stood a crystal palace, for a sailor to admire;
  For a troop of ghosts came round us,
  Which with leaves of bay they crowned us,
Then with grog they well-nigh drowned us, to the depth of
our desire!
And 'twas very friendly of them, as a sailor can admire!

There was music all about us, we were growing quite for-
getful
We were only singing seamen from the dirt of London-town,
Though the nectar that we swallowed seemed to vanish half
regretful
As if we wasn't good enough to take such vittles down,
  When we saw a sudden figure,
  Tall and black as any nigger,
Like the devil—only bigger—drawing near us with a frown!
Like the devil—but much bigger—and he wore a golden
crown!

And "What's all this?" he growls at us! With dignity we
chaunted,
"Forty singing seamen, sir, as won't be put upon!"
"What? Englishmen?" he cries, "Well, if ye don't mind be-
ing haunted,
Faith, you're welcome to my palace; I'm the famous Prester
John!

[32]

Will ye walk into my palace?
I don't bear 'ee any malice!
One and all ye shall be welcome in the halls of Prester John!"
So we walked into the palace and the halls of Prester John!

Now the door was one great diamond and the hall a hollow
    ruby—
Big as Beachy Head, my lads, nay, bigger by a half!
And I sees the mate wi' mouth agape, a-staring like a booby,
And the skipper close behind him, with his tongue out like
    a calf!
    Now the way to take it rightly
    Was to walk along politely
Just as if you didn't notice—so I couldn't help but laugh!
For they both forgot their manners and the crew was bound
    to laugh!

But he took us through his palace, and, my lads, as I'm a
    sinner,
We walked into an opal like a sunset-colored cloud—
"My dining room," he says, and, quick as light, we saw a
    dinner
Spread before us by the fingers of a hidden fairy crowd;
    And the skipper, swaying gently
    After dinner, murmurs faintly,
"I looks to-wards you, Prester John, you've done us very
    proud!"
And he drank his health with honors, for he *done* us *very*
    proud!

Then he walks us to his gardens where we sees a feathered
    demon
Very splendid and important on a sort of spicy tree!
"That's the Phoenix," whispers Prester, "which all eddi-
    cated seamen

Knows the only one existent, and *he's* waiting for to flee!
   When his hundred years expire
   Then he'll set hisself a-fire
And another from his ashes rise most beautiful to see!
With wings of rose and emerald most beautiful to see!

Then he says, "In yonder forest there's a little silver river
And whosoever drinks of it, his youth will never die!
The centuries go by, but Prester John endures for ever
With his music in the mountains and his magic on the sky!
   While *your* hearts are growing colder,
   While your world is growing older,
There's a magic in the distance, where the sea-line meets the
   sky.
It shall call to singing seamen till the fount o' song is dry!"

So we thought we'd up and seek it, but that forest fair de-
   fied us,—
First a crimson leopard laughed at us most horrible to see,
Then a sea-green lion came and sniffed and licked his chops
   and eyed us,
While a red and yellow unicorn was dancing round a tree!
   We was trying to look thinner,
   Which was hard, because our dinner
Must ha' made us very tempting to a cat o' high degree!
Must ha' made us very tempting to the whole menarjeree!

So we scuttled from that forest and across the poppy
   meadows
Where the awful shaggy horror brooded o'er us in the dark!
And we pushes out from shore again a-jumping at our
   shadows
And pulls away most joyful to the old black barque!
   And home again we plodded
   While the Polyphemus nodded

With his battered moon-eye winking red and yellow through
the dark.
Oh, the moon above the mountains red and yellow through
the dark!

Across the seas of Wonderland to London-town we blun-
dered,
Forty singing seamen as was puzzled for to know
If the visions that we saw was caused by—here again we
pondered—
A tipple in a vision forty thousand years ago.
   Could the grog we *dreamt* we swallowed
   Make us *dream* of all that followed?
We were simply singing seamen, so of course we didn't know!
We were simply singing seamen, so of course we could not
know!

THE PIED PIPER OF HAMELIN

ROBERT BROWNING

*Browning knew a boy who had a gift for drawing. He wrote this poem
as a subject for the boy to illustrate. He did not himself think highly of
it and had no intention of publishing it, but some time later the printers
were short of copy in making up one of Browning's books and Browning
put "The Pied Piper" in to fill up. We are glad that he did.*

Hamelin town's in Brunswick,
By famous Hanover city;
The River Weser, deep and wide,
Washes its walls on the southern side;
A pleasanter spot you never spied;
—But, when begins my ditty?
Almost five hundred years ago,
To see the townsfolk suffer so
   From vermin, was a pity.

Rats!
They fought the dogs and killed the cats,
   And bit the babies in the cradles,
And ate the cheeses out of the vats,
   And licked the soup from the cooks' own ladles,
Split open the kegs of salted sprats,
Made nests inside men's Sunday hats,
And even spoiled the women's chats,
   By drowning their speaking
   With shrieking and squeaking
In fifty different sharps and flats.

At last the people in a body
   To the Town Hall came flocking:
" 'Tis clear," cried they, "our Mayor's a noddy,
And as for our Corporation—shocking
To think we buy gowns lined with ermine
For dolts that can't or won't determine
What's best to rid us of our vermin!
You hope, because you're old and obese,
To find in the furry civic robe ease?
Rouse up, Sirs! Give your brains a racking
To find the remedy we're lacking,
Or, sure as fate, we'll send you packing!"
At this the Mayor and Corporation
Quaked with a mighty consternation.

An hour they sate in counsel—
   At length the Mayor broke silence:
"For a guilder I'd my ermine gown sell;
   I wish I were a mile hence!
It's easy to bid one rack one's brain—
I'm sure my poor head aches again,
I've scratched it so, and all in vain.
Oh for a trap, a trap, a trap!"

Just as he said this, what should hap
At the chamber door but a gentle tap.
"Bless us," cried the Mayor, "what's that?"
(With the Corporation as he sat,
Looking little, though wondrous fat;
Nor brighter was his eye, nor moister
Than a too-long-opened oyster,
Save when at noon his paunch grew mutinous
For a plate of turtle, green and glutinous.)
"Only a scraping of shoes on the mat?
Anything like the sound of a rat
Makes my heart go pit-a-pat!"

"Come in!" the Mayor cried, looking bigger,
And in did come the strangest figure!
His queer long coat, from heel to head
Was half of yellow and half of red;
And he himself was tall and thin,
With sharp blue eyes, each like a pin,
And light loose hair, yet swarthy skin,
No tuft on cheek nor beard on chin,
But lips where smiles went out and in;
There was no guessing his kith and kin;
And nobody could enough admire
The tall man and his quaint attire.
Quoth one: "It's as if my great-grandsire,
Starting up at the trump of Doom's tone,
Had walked this way from his painted tombstone!"

He advanced to the council table:
And, "Please your honors," said he, "I'm able,
By means of a secret charm, to draw
All creatures living beneath the sun,
That creep, or swim, or fly, or run,
After me so as you never saw!

And I chiefly use my charm
On creatures that do people harm—
The mole, the toad, the newt, the viper:
And people call me the Pied Piper."

(And here they noticed round his neck
A scarf of red and yellow stripe,
To match with his coat of the self-same check;
And at the scarf's end hung a pipe;
And his fingers, they noticed, were ever straying
As if impatient to be playing
Upon this pipe, as low it dangled
Over his vesture so old-fangled.)
"Yet," said he, "poor piper as I am,
In Tartary I freed the Cham,
Last June, from his huge swarm of gnats;
I eased in Asia the Nizam
Of a monstrous brood of vampire-bats;
And, as for what your brain bewilders
If I can rid your town of rats,
Will you give me a thousand guilders?"
"One? fifty thousand!"—was the exclamation
Of the astonished Mayor and Corporation.

Into the street the Piper stept,
    Smiling first a little smile,
As if he knew what magic slept
    In his quiet pipe the while;
Then, like a musical adept,
To blow the pipe his lips he wrinkled,
And green and blue his sharp eyes twinkled,
Like a candle flame where salt is sprinkled;
And ere three shrill notes the pipe uttered,
You heard as if an army muttered;
And the muttering grew to a grumbling;

And the grumbling grew to a mighty rumbling;
And out of the houses the rats came tumbling.
Great rats, small rats, lean rats, brawny rats,
Brown rats, black rats, grey rats, tawny rats,
Grave old plodders, gay young friskers,
    Fathers, mothers, uncles, cousins,
Cocking tails and pricking whiskers;
    Families by tens and dozens,
Brothers, sisters, husbands, wives—
Followed the Piper for their lives.
From street to street he piped, advancing,
And step for step they followed dancing,
Until they came to the River Weser,
Wherein all plunged and perished!
—Save one, who, stout as Julius Cæsar,
Swam across and lived to carry
(As he, the manuscript he cherished)
To Rat-land home his commentary:
Which was, "At the first shrill note of the pipe
I heard a sound as of scraping tripe,
And putting apples, wondrous ripe,
Into a cider-press's gripe:
And a moving away of pickle-tub boards,
And a leaving ajar of conserve-cupboards,
And a drawing the corks of train-oil-flasks,
And a breaking the hoops of butter-casks:
And it seemed as if a voice
(Sweeter far than by harp or by psaltery
Is breathed) called out, 'Oh, rats, rejoice!
'The world is grown to one vast drysaltery!
'So munch on, crunch on, take your nuncheon.
'Breakfast, dinner, supper, luncheon!'
And just as a bulky sugar-puncheon,
All ready staved, like a great sun shone
Glorious, scarce an inch before me,

[39]

Just as methought it said, 'Come, bore me!'
—I found the Weser rolling o'er me."

You should have heard the Hamelin people
Ringing the bells till they rocked the steeple;
"Go," cried the Mayor, "and get long poles!
Poke out the nests and block up the holes!
Consult with carpenters and builders,
And leave in our town not even a trace
Of the rats!"—when suddenly up the face
Of the Piper perked in the market-place,
With a "First, if you please, my thousand guilders!"

A thousand guilders! The Mayor looked blue;
So did the Corporation too.
For council dinners made rare havoc
With Claret, Moselle, Vin-de-Grave, Hock;
And half the money would replenish
Their cellar's biggest butt with Rhenish.
To pay this sum to a wandering fellow
With a gipsy coat of red and yellow!
"Beside," quoth the Mayor, with a knowing wink,
"Our business was done at the river's brink;
We saw with our eyes the vermin sink,
And what's dead can't come to life, I think.
So, friend, we're not the folks to shrink
From the duty of giving you something for drink,
And a matter of money to put in your poke;
But, as for the guilders, what we spoke
Of them, as you very well know, was in joke.
Beside, our losses have made us thrifty;
A thousand guilders! Come, take fifty!"

The piper's face fell, and he cried,
"No trifling! I can't wait! beside,

I've promised to visit by dinner time
Bagdat, and accept the prime
Of the Head-Cook's pottage, all he's rich in,
For having left, in the Caliph's kitchen,
Of a nest of scorpions no survivor.
With him I proved no bargain-driver;
With you, don't think I'll bate a stiver!
And folks who put me in a passion
May find me pipe after another fashion."

"How!" cried the Mayor, "d'ye think I'll brook
Being worse treated than a Cook?
Insulted by a lazy ribald
With idle pipe and vesture piebald!
You threaten us, fellow! Do your worst;
Blow your pipe there till you burst!"

Once more he stept into the street,
    And to his lips again
Laid his long pipe of smooth, straight cane;
    And ere he blew three notes (such sweet
Soft notes as yet musician's cunning
    Never gave the enraptured air)
There was a rustling that seemed like a bustling
Of merry crowds justling at pitching and hustling,
Small feet were pattering, wooden shoes clattering,
Little hands clapping, and little tongues chattering;
And, like fowls in a farm-yard when barley is scattering,
Out came the children running.
All the little boys and girls,
With rosy cheeks and flaxen curls,
And sparkling eyes and teeth like pearls,
Tripping and skipping, ran merrily after
The wonderful music with shouting and laughter.
The Mayor was dumb, and the Council stood

As if they were changed into blocks of wood,
Unable to move a step, or cry
To the children merrily skipping by—
And could only follow with the eye
That joyous crowd at the Piper's back.
But how the Mayor was on the rack,
And the wretched Council's bosoms beat,
As the Piper turned from the High Street
To where the Weser rolled its waters
Right in the way of their sons and daughters!
However, he turned from South to West,
And to Koppelberg Hill his steps addressed,
And after him the children pressed;
Great was the joy in every breast.
"He never can cross that mighty top!
He's forced to let the piping drop,
And we shall see our children stop!"
When lo, as they reached the mountain's side,
A wondrous portal opened wide,
As if a cavern was suddenly hollowed;
And the Piper advanced and the children followed;
And when all were in, to the very last,
The door in the mountain side shut fast.
Did I say all? No! One was lame,
And could not dance the whole of the way!
And in after years, if you would blame
His sadness, he used to say,—
"It's dull in our town since my playmates left!
I can't forget that I'm bereft
Of all the pleasant sights they see,
Which the Piper also promised me:
For he led us, he said, to a joyous land,
Joining the town and just at hand,
Where waters gushed and fruit trees grew,
And flowers put forth a fairer hue,
And everything was strange and new;

The sparrows were brighter than peacocks here,
And their dogs outran our fallow-deer,
And honey-bees had lost their stings,
And horses were born with eagles' wings:
And just as I became assured
My lame foot would be speedily cured,
The music stopped, and I stood still,
And found myself outside the hill,
Left alone against my will,
To go now limping as before,
And never hear of that country more!"

Alas, alas for Hamelin!
   There came into many a burgher's pate
   A text which says that Heaven's gate
   Opes to the rich at as easy rate
As the needle's eye takes a camel in!
The Mayor sent East, West, North, and South,
To offer the Piper, by word of mouth,
   Wherever it was man's lot to find him,
Silver and gold to his heart's content,
If he'd only return the way he went,
   And bring the children behind him.
But when they saw 'twas a lost endeavor,
And Piper and dancers were gone for ever,
They made a decree that lawyers never
   Should think their records dated duly
If, after the day of the month and the year,
These words did not as well appear,
"And so long after what happened here
On the Twenty-second of July,
Thirteen hundred and seventy-six":
And the better in memory to fix
The place of the children's last retreat,
They called it, the Pied Piper's Street—
Where any one playing on pipe or tabor

Was sure for the future to lose his labor.
Nor suffered they hostelry or tavern
   To shock with mirth a street so solemn;
But opposite the place of the cavern
   They wrote the story on a column,
And on the Great Church window painted
The same, to make the world acquainted
How their children were stolen away;
And there it stands to this very day.
And I must not omit to say
That in Transylvania there's a tribe
Of alien people, that ascribe
The outlandish ways and dress
On which their neighbors lay such stress
To their fathers and mothers having risen
Out of some subterranean prison,
Into which they were trepanned
Long time ago, in a mighty band,
Out of Hamelin town in Brunswick land,
But how or why, they don't understand.

So, Willy, let you and me be wipers
Of scores out with all men—especially pipers:
And, whether they pipe us free from rats or from mice,
If we promised them aught, let us keep our promise.

THE LISTENERS

WALTER DE LA MARE

Is there anybody there?" said the Traveller,
   Knocking on the moonlit door;
And his horse in the silence champed the grasses
   Of the forest's ferny floor:

And a bird flew up out of the turret,
    Above the Traveller's head:
And he smote upon the door again a second time;
    "Is there anybody there?" he said.
But no one descended to the Traveller;
    No head from the leaf-fringed sill
Leaned over and looked into his grey eyes,
    Where he stood perplexed and still.
But only a host of phantom listeners
    That dwelt in the lone house then
Stood listening in the quiet of the moonlight
    To that voice from the world of men:
Stood thronging the faint moon beams on the dark stair,
    That goes down to the empty hall,
Hearkening in an air stirred and shaken
    By the lonely Traveller's call.
And he felt in his heart their strangeness,
    Their stillness answering his cry,
While his horse moved, cropping the dark turf,
    'Neath the starred and leafy sky;
For he suddenly smote on the door, even
    Louder, and lifted his head:—
"Tell them I came, and no one answered,
    That I kept my word," he said.
Never the least stir made the listeners,
    Though every word he spake
Fell echoing through the shadowiness of the still house
    From the one man left awake:
Ay, they heard his foot upon the stirrup,
    And the sound of iron on stone
And how the silence surged softly backward
    When the plunging hoofs were gone.

EDWARD, EDWARD

ANONYMOUS

This is one of the best samples of the English popular ballad. It was probably first made by some wandering singer and passed down from generation to generation by word of mouth. Percy, the famous collector of ballads, first published it in 1765. The same ballad, in somewhat varied form, is found in the Swedish, Danish and Finnish.

Why does your brand sae drop wi' blude,
    Edward, Edward?
Why does your brand sae drop wi' blude,
    And why sae sad gang ye, O?"
"O I hae kill'd my hawk sae gude,
    Mither, mither;
O I hae kill'd my hawk sae gude,
    And I had nae mair but he, O."

"Your hawk's blude was never sae red,
    Edward, Edward;
Your hawk's blude was never sae red,
    My dear son, I tell thee, O."
"O I hae kill'd my red-roan steed,
    Mither, mither;
O I hae kill'd my red-roan steed,
    That erst was sae fair and free, O."

"Your steed was auld, and ye hae got mair,
    Edward, Edward;
Your steed was auld, and ye hae got mair,
    Some other dule ye dree, O."
"O I hae kill'd my father dear,
    Mither, mither;
O I hae kill'd my father dear,
    Alas, and wae is me, O!"

"And whatten penance will ye dree for that,
   Edward, Edward?
Whatten penance will ye dree for that?
   My dear son, now tell me, O."
"I'll set my feet in yonder boat,
   Mither, mither;
I'll set my feet in yonder boat,
   And I'll fare over the sea, O."

And what will ye do wi' your tow'rs and your ha',
   Edward, Edward?
And what will ye do wi' your tow'rs and your ha',
   That were sae fair to see, O?"
"I'll let them stand till they down fa',
   Mither, mither;
I'll let them stand till they down fa',
   For here never mair maun I be, O."

"And what will ye leave to your bairns and your wife,
   Edward, Edward?
And what will ye leave to your bairns and your wife,
   When ye gang owre the sea, O?"
"The warld's room: let them beg through life,
   Mither, mither;
The warld's room: let them beg through life;
   For them never mair will I see, O."

"And what will ye leave to your ain mither dear,
   Edward, Edward?
And what will ye leave to your ain mither dear,
   My dear son, now tell me, O?"
"The curse of hell frae me sall ye bear,
   Mither, mither;
The curse of hell frae me sall ye bear:
   Sic counsels ye gave to me, O!"

LA BELLE DAME SANS MERCI

JOHN KEATS

O what can ail thee, knight-at-arms,
Alone and palely loitering?
The sedge has withered from the lake,
And no birds sing.

O what can ail thee, knight-at-arms,
So haggard and so woe-begone?
The squirrel's granary is full,
And the harvest's done.

I see a lily on thy brow
With anguish moist and fever dew,
And on thy cheek a fading rose
Fast withereth too.

I met a lady in the meads,
Full beautiful—a faery's child,
Her hair was long, her foot was light,
And her eyes were wild.

I made a garland for her head,
And bracelets, too, and fragrant zone;
She looked at me as she did love,
And made sweet moan.

I set her on my pacing steed,
And nothing else saw all day long,
For sidelong would she bend, and sing,
A faery's song.

She found me roots of relish sweet,
And honey wild, and manna dew,
And sure in language strange she said—
"I love thee true."

She took me to her elfin grot,
And there she wept and sighed full sore,
And there I shut her wild, wild eyes
With kisses four.

And there she lullèd me asleep,
And there I dreamed—ah, woe betide.
The latest dream I ever dream'd
On the cold hill's side.

I saw pale kings and princes too,
Pale warriors, death pale were they all;
They cried—"La Belle Dame sans Merci
Hath thee in thrall."

I saw their starved lips in the gloom,
With horrid warning gapèd wide,
And I awoke and found me here,
On the cold hill's side.

And this is why I sojourn here,
Alone and palely loitering,
Though the sedge is wither'd from the lake
And no birds sing.

Keats was apprenticed at fifteen to a surgeon in London. He kept at the work for some years but he was not suited to the profession and resolved to be a writer. In four short years all his literary work was done, for he died in Italy at the age of twenty-six.

WILLIAM I—1066

ELEANOR FARJEON

William the First was the first of our kings,
Not counting Ethelreds, Egberts and things,
And he had himself crowned and anointed and blest
In Ten-Sixty-I-Needn't-Tell-You-The-Rest.

But being a Norman, King William the First
By the Saxons he conquered was hated and cursed,
And they planned and they plotted far into the night,
Which William could tell by the candles alight.

Then William decided these rebels to quell
By ringing the Curfew, a sort of a bell,
And if any Saxon was found out of bed
After eight o'clock sharp, it was Off With His Head!

So at BONG NUMBER ONE they all started to run
Like a warren of rabbits upset by a gun;
At BONG NUMBER TWO they were all in a stew,
Flinging cap after tunic and hose after shoe;
At BONG NUMBER THREE they were bare to the knee,
Undoing the doings as quick as could be;
At BONG NUMBER FOUR they were stripped to the core,
And pulling on nightshirts the wrong side before;
At BONG NUMBER FIVE they were looking alive,
And bizzing and buzzing like bees in a hive;
At BONG NUMBER SIX they gave themselves kicks,
Tripping over the rushes to snuff out the wicks;
At BONG NUMBER SEVEN, from Durham to Devon,
They slipped up a prayer to Our Father in Heaven;

And at BONG NUMBER EIGHT it was fatal to wait,
So with hearts beating all at a terrible rate,
In the deuce of a state, I need hardly relate,
They jumped BONG into bed like a bull at a gate.

This is the first of Miss Farjeon's delightful series of verses about each king and queen of English history, in meters and moods to suit their characters and their times.

THE ENCHANTED SHIRT

JOHN HAY

The king was sick. His cheek was red,
  And his eye was clear and bright;
He ate and drank with kingly zest,
  And peacefully snored at night.

But he said he was sick and a king should know,
  And the doctors came by the score.
They did not cure him. He cut off their heads,
  And sent to the schools for more.

At last two famous doctors came,
  And one was as poor as a rat,—
He had passed his life in studious toil,
  And never found time to grow fat.

The other had never looked in a book;
  His patients gave him no trouble:
If they recovered, they paid him well;
  If they died, their heirs paid double.

Together they looked at the royal tongue,
  As the king on his couch reclined;
In succession they thumped his august chest,
  But no trace of disease could find.

The old Sage said, "You're as sound as a nut."
  "Hang him up," roared the king in a gale—
In a ten-knot gale of royal rage;
  The other leech grew a shade pale;

But he pensively rubbed his sagacious nose,
  And thus his prescription ran—
The king will be well, if he sleeps one night
  In the shirt of a Happy Man.

Wide o'er the realm the couriers rode,
  And fast their horses ran,
And many they saw, and to many they spoke,
  But they found no Happy Man.

They found poor men who would fain be rich,
  And rich who thought they were poor;
And men who twisted their waists in stays,
  And women who short hose wore.

At last they came to a village gate,
  A beggar lay whistling there;
He whistled, and sang, and laughed, and rolled
  On the grass, in the soft June air.

The weary couriers paused and looked
  At the scamp so blithe and gay;
And one of them said, "Heaven save you, friend!
  You seem to be happy to-day."

"O yes, fair Sirs," the rascal laughed,
　And his voice rang free and glad;
"An idle man has so much to do
　That he never has time to be sad."

"This is our man," the courier said;
　"Our luck has led us aright.
I will give you a hundred ducats, friend,
　For the loan of your shirt to-night."

The merry blackguard lay back on the grass,
　And laughed till his face was black;
"I would do it, God wot," and he roared with the fun,
　"But I haven't a shirt to my back."

Each day to the king the reports came in
　Of his unsuccessful spies,
And the sad panorama of human woes
　Passed daily under his eyes.

And he grew ashamed of his useless life,
　And his maladies hatched in gloom;
He opened his windows and let the air
　Of the free heaven into his room.

And out he went in the world, and toiled
　In his own appointed way;
And the people blessed him, the land was glad,
　And the king was well and gay.

LOCHINVAR

WALTER SCOTT

Oh, young Lochinvar is come out of the west.
Through all the wide Border his steed was the best,
And save his good broadsword he weapons had none;
He rode all unarmed, and he rode all alone.
So faithful in love, and so dauntless in war,
There never was knight like the young Lochinvar.

He stayed not for brake, and he stopped not for stone,
He swam the Eske River where ford there was none:
But ere he alighted at Netherby gate
The bride had consented, the gallant came late:
For a laggard in love, and a dastard in war
Was to wed the fair Ellen of brave Lochinvar.

So boldly he entered the Netherby Hall,
Among bridesmen and kinsmen and brothers and all:
Then spoke the bride's father, his hand on his sword
(For the poor craven bridegroom said never a word),
"O come ye in peace here, or come ye in war,
Or to dance at our bridal, young Lord Lochinvar?"

"I long wooed your daughter, my suit you denied—
Love swells like the Solway, but ebbs like its tide—
And now I am come, with this lost love of mine,
To lead but one measure, drink one cup of wine;
There are maidens in Scotland more lovely by far,
That would gladly be bride to the young Lochinvar."

The bride kissed the goblet—the knight took it up;
He quaffed off the wine, and he threw down the cup,
She looked down to blush, and she looked up to sigh,
With a smile on her lips, and a tear in her eye.

He took her soft hand, ere her mother could bar—
"Now, tread we a measure!" said young Lochinvar.

So stately his form, and so lovely her face,
That never a hall such a galliard did grace;
While her mother did fret and her father did fume,
And the bridegroom stood dangling his bonnet and plume;
And the bride-maidens whispered, " 'Twere better by far
To have matched our fair cousin with young Lochinvar."

One touch to her hand, and one word in her ear,
When they reached the hall door, and the charger stood
    near;
So light to the croup the fair lady he swung,
So light to the saddle before her he sprung!
"She is won! we are gone, over bank, bush, and scaur;
They'll have fleet steeds that follow," quoth young Lochin-
    var.

There was mounting 'mong Græmes of the Netherby clan;
Forsters, Fenwicks, and Musgraves, they rode and they ran:
There was racing and chasing on Cannobie Lea,
But the lost bride of Netherby ne'er did they see.
So daring in love, and so dauntless in war,
Have ye e'er heard of gallant like young Lochinvar?

THE SAILOR'S CONSOLATION

CHARLES DIBDIN

One night came on a hurricane,
    The sea was mountains rolling
When Barney Buntline turned his quid
    And said to Billy Bowling,
"A strong nor'wester's blowing, Bill;

Hark! don't ye hear it roar, now?
    Lord help 'em, how I pities them
        Unhappy folks on shore now!

"Foolhardy chaps who live in towns,
    What danger they are all in,
And now lie quaking in their beds,
    For fear the roof should fall in;
Poor creatures! how they envies us,
    And wishes, I've a notion,
For our good luck, in such a storm,
    To be upon the ocean!

"And as for them who are out all day
    On business from their houses,
And late at night are coming home,
    To cheer their babes and spouses,—
While you and I, Bill, on the deck
    Are comfortably lying,
My eyes! what tiles and chimney-pots
    About their heads are flying!

"And very often have we heard
    How men are killed and undone
By overturns of carriages,
    By thieves and fires in London;
We know what risks all landsmen run,
    From noblemen to tailors;
Then, Bill, let's us thank Providence
    That you and I are sailors."

Dibdin was an English ballad writer of the eighteenth century. He never went to sea himself, but his favorite brother was a sea captain and he wrote hundreds of sea songs which were very popular among seamen.

DERELICT

A Reminiscence of R. L. S.'s "Treasure Island"

YOUNG E. ALLISON

Few people know that "The Dead Man's Chest" is the name of a treacherous sunken reef in the Caribbean Sea. The legend on which this poem is based is that a Spanish treasure galleon was raided by a pirate crew, who fell to fighting over the division of the loot. The result of this fight was that fifteen husky cutthroats set their companions adrift in the longboat, and, still unable to agree among themselves, started a second fight that resulted in the death of all. The galleon drifted derelict on the Dead Man's Chest, where she was later discovered by the crew who had been set adrift. It is the bosun's mate who tells of the sight that met their eyes as they clambered up the side.

Fifteen men on the dead man's chest—
    "Yo-ho-ho and a bottle of rum!
"Drink and the devil had done for the rest—
    "Yo-ho-ho and a bottle of rum!"
The mate was fixed by the bos'n's pike,
The bos'n brained with a marlinspike
And Cookey's throat was marked belike
      It had been gripped
      By fingers ten;
    And there they lay,
      All good dead men,
Like break-o'-day in a boozing-ken—
    Yo-ho-ho and a bottle of rum!

Fifteen men of a whole ship's list—
    Yo-ho-ho and a bottle of rum!
Dead and bedamned and the rest gone whist!—
    Yo-ho-ho and a bottle of rum!
The skipper lay with his nob in gore

Where the scullion's axe his cheek had shore—
And the scullion he was stabbed times four.
    And there they lay
      And the soggy skies
    Dripped all day long
      In up-staring eyes—
At murk sunset and at foul sunrise—
    Yo-ho-ho and a bottle of rum!

Fifteen men of 'em stiff and stark—
    Yo-ho-ho and a bottle of rum!
Ten of the crew had the Murder mark—
    Yo-ho-ho and a bottle of rum!
'Twas a cutlass swipe, or an ounce of lead,
Or a yawning hole in a battered head—
And the scuppers glut with a rotting red.
    And there they lay—
      Aye, damn my eyes!—
    All lookouts clapped
      On paradise—
All souls bound just contrariwise—
    Yo-ho-ho and a bottle of rum!

Fifteen men of 'em good and true—
    Yo-ho-ho and a bottle of rum!
Every man jack could ha' sailed with Old Pew—
    Yo-ho-ho and a bottle of rum!
There was chest on chest full of Spanish gold,
With a ton of plate in the middle hold,
And the cabins riot of stuff untold,
    And they lay there,
      That had took the plum,
    With sightless glare
      And their eyes struck dumb,
While we shared all by the rule of thumb—
    Yo-ho-ho and a bottle of rum!

More was seen through the sternlight screen—
    Yo-ho-ho and a bottle of rum!
Chartings no doubt where a woman had been!—
    Yo-ho-ho and a bottle of rum!
A flimsy shift on a bunker cot,
With a thin dirt slot through the bosom spot
And the lace stiff-dry in a purplish blot.
    Or was she wench . . .
        Or some shuddering maid . . . ?
    That dared the knife—
        And that took the blade!
By God! she was stuff for a plucky jade—
    Yo-ho-ho and a bottle of rum!

"Fifteen men on the dead man's chest—
    "Yo-ho-ho and a bottle of rum!
"Drink and the devil had done for the rest—
    "Yo-ho-ho and a bottle of rum!"
We wrapped 'em all in a mains'l tight,
With twice ten turns of a hawser's bight,
And we heaved 'em over and out of sight—
    With a yo-heave-ho!
        And a fare-you-well!
    And a sullen plunge
        In the sullen swell
Ten fathoms deep on the road to hell!
    Yo-ho-ho and a bottle of rum!

PEG-LEG'S FIDDLE

BILL ADAMS

I've a pal called Billy Peg-Leg, with one leg a wood leg,
And Billy he's a ship's cook, and lives upon the sea;
And, hanging by his griddle,
Old Billy keeps a fiddle,
For fiddling in the dog-watch, when the moon is on the sea.

We takes our luck wi' tough ships, wi' fast ships, wi' free
    ships,
We takes our luck wi' any ship to sign away for sea;
We takes our trick wi' the best o' them,
And sings our song wi' the rest o' them,
When the bell strikes the dog-watch, and the moon is on the
    sea.

You'd ought to see them top'sls, them stays'ls, them stuns'ls,
When the moon's a-shinin' on them along a liftin' sea;
Hear the dandy bo'sun say,
"Peg-Leg, make that fiddle play,
And we'll dance away the dog-watch, while the moon is on
    the sea."

Then it's fun to see them dancin',—them bow-legged sailors
    dancin',
To the tune o' Peg-Leg's fiddle, a-fiddlin' fast and free,
It's fun to watch old Peg-Leg,
A'waltzin' wi' his wood leg,
When bo'sun takes the fiddle, so Peg can dance wi' me.

The moon is on the water, the dark moon-glimmered water,
The night wind pipin' plaintively along a liftin' sea;
There ain't no female wimmen,

No big beer glasses brimmin',
There's just the great sea's glory, an' Billy Peg an' me.

We takes our luck wi' tough ships, wi' fast ships, wi' free
    ships,
We takes our luck wi' any ship to sign away to sea;
We takes our trick wi' the best o' them,
And sings our song wi' the rest o' them,
When the bell strikes the dog-watch, and the moon is on the
    sea.

*Bill Adams was heart and soul a man of the sea. He went to sea as a
boy and had thrilling experiences on Cape Horn voyages in the days of
"wooden ships and iron men."*

THE BALLAD OF THE *IVANHOE*

BILL ADAMS

What is she making?" asked the mate;
"She's making her sixteen, sir."
"One hundred days to the Golden Gate,"
Said the hard-case mate,—
The *Ivanhoe* was running for the open sea.

"What's she making?" asked the skipper;
"Still logging her sixteen, sir."
"Two more nights and she'll lose the dipper,"
Muttered her skipper,—
And the *Ivanhoe* was whooping it southerly.

"What's she makin', bullies?" asked Chips;
"Sixteen knots on her course, lad."
"Then she'll whip them lubberly London ships,"

Grinned Carpenter Chips.—
And then the Pampero caught her under full sail.

"She's lost one whole storm suit," said Sails,
They fetched new from the locker
And dressed her from boom to her spanker brails
For the Cape Horn gales,—
And then old *Ivanhoe* ran southing toward the Horn.

"Seen no sun in a month," growled Bose,
"A full Horn gale's a-blowin',
An' all of her yards is jammed up close,
My Gawd!—'*ow it snows!*"
Old *Ivanhoe* had been a full four weeks off Stiff.

"Where's the skipper?" the froze mate said,
"I haven't seen him of late."
"He's overboard, and he's drowned and dead,"
And, shaking his head,
"You'll have to sail her to 'Frisco," said the second.

"Wot was it crashed in the black night?"
"Her topmasts carried away!"
"My word, but ain't it blowin' a fright?
Oh, Gawd fer th' light!"
And that was when she'd been six weeks off old Cape Stiff.

Six men lay dead. Calm came in spells.
The second mate went crazy;
Old *Ivanhoe* lifted to the swells
Clanging both her bells,—
Her wreckage trailed astern amidst the Cape Horn bergs.

"What is she making?" asked the mate.
"Just creeping at two knots, sir."
"Three hundred days to the Golden Gate,"

Said her hard-case mate,—
When a fair wind blew after eight weeks off Cape Stiff.

"Will we sail into Vallapo
For refittin'?" asked the hands.
"No, sons! *Not by a hell of a show!*
We will take her so,
Just as she is, to 'Frisco," said her hard-case mate.

"A steamer's comin' through the swell,
Offerin' us assistance."
"Signal the lubber to go to hell!
Signal him, 'All's well.' "
Old Ivanhoe had been two hundred days at sea.

"What's come of that old *Ivanhoe?*"
Asked one of the clerks at Lloyd's,
"Perished, maybe, in a Cape Horn blow,
There's none to know!"
And then they slowly tolled the bell for her at Lloyd's.

Jury rigged, with all her freight,
And the red rust on her sides,
Came *Ivanhoe,* a twelvemonth late,
With her hard-case mate,
And half her crew, slow stealing through the Golden Gate.

CHRISTMAS AT SEA

ROBERT LOUIS STEVENSON

The sheets were frozen hard, and they cut the naked hand;
The decks were like a slide, where a seaman scarce could
stand;
The wind was a nor'wester, blowing squally off the sea;
And cliffs and spouting breakers were the only things a-lee.

They heard the surf a-roaring before the break of day;
But 'twas only with the peep of light we saw how ill we lay.
We tumbled every man on deck instanter, with a shout,
And we gave her the maintops'l, and stood by to go about.

All day we tacked and tacked between the South Head and
    the North;
All day we hauled the frozen sheets, and got no further
    forth;
All day as cold as charity, in bitter pain and dread,
For very life and nature, we tacked from head to head.

We gave the South a wider berth, for there the tide-race
    roared;
And every tack we made brought the North Head close
    aboard:
So's we saw the cliffs and houses, and the breakers running
    high,
And the coastguard in his garden, with his glass against his
    eye.

The frost was on the village roofs as white as ocean foam;
The good red fires were burning bright in every 'longshore
    home;
The windows sparkled clear, and the chimneys volleyed out;
And I vow we sniffed the victuals as the vessel went about.

The bells upon the church were rung with a mighty jovial
    cheer
For it's just that I should tell you how (of all days of the
    year)
This day of our adversity was blessèd Christmas morn,
And the house above the coastguard's was the house where
    I was born.

O well I saw the pleasant room, the pleasant faces there,
My mother's silver spectacles, my father's silver hair;
And well I saw the firelight, like a flock of homely elves,
Go dancing round the china-plates that stand upon the
shelves.

And well I knew the talk they had, the talk that was of me,
Of the shadow on the household, and the son that went to
sea;
And oh, the wicked fool I seemed, in every kind of way,
To be here and hauling frozen ropes, on blessèd Christmas
Day.

They lit the high sea-light, and the dark began to fall.
"All hands to loose topgallant sails!" I heard the captain
call,
"By the Lord, she'll never stand it," our first mate, Jackson,
cried.
. . . "It's the one way or the other, Mr. Jackson," he re-
plied.

She staggered to her bearings, but her sails were new and
good.
And the ship smelt up to windward, just as if she understood.
As the winter's day was ending, in the entry of the night,
We cleared the weary headland and passed below the light.

And they heaved a mighty breath, every soul on board
but me,
As they saw her nose again pointing handsome out to sea;
But all that I could think of, in the darkness and the cold,
Was just that I was leaving home, and my folks were grow-
ing old.

THE DAUBER ROUNDS CAPE HORN *

JOHN MASEFIELD

"Dauber" is a splendid sea-story in verse which every boy ought to know. The Dauber was an English boy who ran away to sea, was tortured by the men, but he made a sailor and a brave end. This is a small part of the whole poem.

Then came the cry of "Call all hands on deck!"
The Dauber knew its meaning; it was come:
Cape Horn, that tramples beauty into wreck,
And crumples steel, and smites the strong man dumb.
Down clattered flying kites and staysails: some
Sang out in quick, high calls: the fairleads skirled,
And from the southwest came the end of the world!

. . . .

"Now tumble out, my sons: on deck, here, quick!
Rouse out, away, and come and climb the stick.
I'm going to call the half-deck. Bosun! Hey!
Both topsails coming in. Heave out! Away!"

He went; the Dauber tumbled from his bunk,
Clutching the side. He heard the wind go past,
Making the great ship wallow as if drunk.
There was a shocking tumult up the mast.
"This is the end," he muttered, "come at last.
I've got to go aloft, facing this cold.
I can't. I can't. I'll never keep my hold."

And then the thought came: I'm a failure. All
My life has been a failure. They were right.
It will not matter if I go and fall;
I should be free then from this hell's delight.

* Reprinted from Masefield's "Story of a Round House." By special arrangement with the Macmillan Company.

I'll never paint. Best let it end to-night.
I'll slip over the side. I've tried and failed."
So in the ice-cold in the night he quailed.

And then he bit his lips, clenching his mind,
And staggered out to muster, beating back
The coward frozen self of him that whined.
Come what cards might, he meant to play the pack.
"Ai!" screamed the wind; the topsail sheet went clack;
Ice filled the air with spikes; the graybacks burst.
"Here's Dauber," said the Mate, "on deck the first."

. . . .

So up upon the topsail yard again,
In the great tempest's fiercest hour, began
Probation to the Dauber's soul, of pain
Which crowds a century's torment in a span.
For the next month the ocean taught this man,
And he, in that month's torment, while she wested,
Was never warm nor dry, nor full nor rested.

A great gray sea was running up the sky,
Desolate birds flew past; their mewings came
As that lone water's spiritual cry,
Its forlorn voice, its essence, its soul's name.
The ship limped in the water as if lame;
Then in the forenoon watch to a great shout
More sail was made, the reefs were shaken out.

Slowly the sea went down as the wind fell.
Clear rang the songs, "Hurrah! Cape Horn is bet!"
The combless seas were lumping into swell;
The leaking fo'c'sles were no longer wet.
More sail was made; the watch on deck was set
To cleaning up the ruin broken bare
Below, aloft, about her, everywhere.

[67]

The Dauber, scrubbing out the round-house, found
Old pantiles pulped among the mouldy gear,
Washed underneath the bunks and long since drowned
During the agony of the Cape Horn year.
He sang in scrubbing, for he had done with fear—
Fronted the worst and looked it in the face;
He had got manhood at the testing-place.

THE THREE FISHERS

CHARLES KINGSLEY

Three fishers went sailing down to the west,
  Away to the west as the sun went down;
Each thought of the woman who loved him the best,
  And the children stood watching them out of the town:
    For men must work, and women must weep,
    And there's little to earn, and many to keep,
Though the harbor bar be moaning.

Three wives sat up in the light-house tower,
  And trimmed the lamps as the sun went down;
And they looked at the squall, and they looked at the shower,
  While the night-rack came rolling up ragged and brown;
    But men must work, and women must weep,
    Though storms be sudden, and waters deep,
And the harbor bar be moaning.

Three corpses lay out on the shining sands,
  In the morning gleam as the tide went down,
And the women are weeping, and wringing their hands,
  For those who will never come home to the town.
    For men must work, and women must weep,
    And the sooner it's over, the sooner to sleep,
And good-bye to the bar and its moaning.

LORRAINE LORÈE

CHARLES KINGSLEY

Are you ready for your steeple-chase, Lorraine, Lorraine,
  Lorèe?
  Barum, Barum, Barum, Barum, Barum, Barum, Baree.
You're booked to ride your capping race today at Coulterlee,
You're booked to ride Vindictive, for all the world to see,
To keep him straight, and keep him first, and win the run
  for me."
  Barum, Barum, Barum, Barum, Barum, Barum, Baree.

She clasped her new-born baby, poor Lorraine, Lorraine,
  Lorèe,
  Barum, Barum, Barum, Barum, Barum, Barum, Baree.
"I cannot ride Vindictive as any man might see,
And I will not ride Vindictive with this baby on my knee;
He's killed a boy and he's killed a man, and why must he
  kill me?"

"Unless you ride Vindictive, Lorraine, Lorraine, Lorèe,
Unless you ride Vindictive today at Coulterlee,
And land him safe across the brook and win the blank for me,
It's you may keep your baby, for you'll get no keep from me."

"That husbands could be cruel," said Lorraine, Lorraine,
  Lorèe,
  "That husbands could be cruel, I have known for seasons
    three;
But oh! to ride Vindictive while a baby cries for me,
And be killed across a fence at last for all the world to see!"

She mastered young Vindictive—Oh! the gallant lass was
  she,
And kept him straight and won the race as near as near
  could be;

But he killed her at the brook against a pollard willow tree,
Oh! he killed her at the brook, the brute, for all the world
    to see.
And no one but the baby cried for poor Lorraine, Lorèe.

*In Victorian days in England women sometimes rode as jockeys in the
dangerous sport of steeplechase. Lorraine Lorèe was one of these and
Kingsley, hearing her story, made it into a poem.*

ANNABEL LEE

EDGAR ALLAN POE

It was many and many a year ago,
    In a kingdom by the sea,
That a maiden there lived whom you may know
    By the name of Annabel Lee;
And this maiden she lived with no other thought
    Than to love and be loved by me.

I was a child and *she* was a child,
    In this kingdom by the sea:
But we loved with a love that was more than love—
    I and my Annabel Lee;
With a love that the wingèd seraphs of heaven
    Coveted her and me.

And this was the reason that, long ago,
    In this kingdom by the sea,
A wind blew out of a cloud, chilling
    My beautiful Annabel Lee;
So that her highborn kinsmen came
    And bore her away from me,
To shut her up in a sepulchre
    In this kingdom by the sea.

The angels, not half so happy in heaven,
    Went envying her and me—
Yes!—that was the reason (as all men know,
    In this kingdom by the sea)
That the wind came out of the cloud by night,
    Chilling and killing my Annabel Lee.

But our love it was stronger by far than the love
    Of those who were older than we—
    Of many far wiser than we—
And neither the angels in heaven above,
    Nor the demons down under the sea,
Can ever dissever my soul from the soul
    Of the beautiful Annabel Lee:

For the moon never beams, without bringing me dreams
    Of the beautiful Annabel Lee;
And the stars never rise, but I feel the bright eyes
    Of the beautiful Annabel Lee;
And so, all the night-tide, I lie down by the side
Of my darling,—my darling,—my life and my bride,
    In her sepulchre there by the sea,
    In her tomb by the side of the sea.

Edgar Allan Poe had, on the whole, a hard and bitter life. At twenty-six he married a beautiful girl of fifteen and was very happy for a time, but in a few years she died. Doubtless this girl wife, Virginia, was the original of Annabel Lee of the poem written some years later.

THE KING OF DENMARK'S RIDE

CAROLINE NORTON

Word was brought to the Danish king,
            (Hurry!)
That the love of his heart lay suffering,
And pined for the comfort his voice would bring.
        (Oh! ride as if you were flying!)
Better he loves each golden curl
On the brow of that Scandinavian girl
Than his rich crown-jewels of ruby and pearl;
        And his Rose of the Isles is dying!

Thirty nobles saddled with speed;
            (Hurry!)
Each one mounted a gallant steed
Which he kept for battle and days of need;
        (Oh! ride as though you were flying!)
Spurs were struck in the foaming flank,
Worn-out chargers staggered and sank;
Bridles were slackened and girths were burst;
But, ride as they would, the king rode first,
        For his Rose of the Isles lay dying.

His nobles are beaten, one by one;
            (Hurry!)
They have fainted, and faltered, and homeward gone;
His little fair page now follows alone,
        For strength and for courage trying.
The king looked back at that faithful child,
Wan was the face that answering smiled.
They passed the drawbridge with clattering din,
Then he dropped, and only the king rode in
        Where his Rose of the Isles lay dying.

The king blew a blast on his bugle-horn,
  (Silence!)
No answer came, but faint and forlorn
An echo returned on the cold gray morn,
Like the breath of a spirit sighing;
The castle portal stood grimly wide;
None welcomed the king from that weary ride!
For dead, in the light of the dawning day,
The pale sweet form of the welcomer lay,
  Who had yearned for his voice while dying!

The panting steed, with a drooping crest,
  Stood weary.
The king returned from her chamber of rest,
The thick sobs choking in his breast;
  And, that dumb companion eying,
The tears gushed forth which he strove to check;
He bowed his head on his charger's neck:
"O steed, that every nerve didst strain,
Dear steed, our ride hath been in vain,
  To the halls where my love lay dying!"

BEDOUIN LOVE SONG

BAYARD TAYLOR

From the desert I come to thee
On a stallion shod with fire;
And the winds are left behind
In the speed of my desire.
Under thy window I stand,
And the midnight hears my cry;
I love thee, I love but thee,
With a love that shall not die

Till the sun grows cold,
And the stars are old,
And the leaves of the Judgment Book unfold.

Look from thy window and see
My passion and my pain;
I lie on the sands below,
And I faint in thy disdain.
Let the night-winds touch thy brow
With the heat of my burning sigh,
And melt thee to hear the vow
Of a love that shall not die
    Till the sun grows cold,
    And the stars are old,
    And the leaves of the Judgment Book unfold.

My steps are nightly driven
By the fever in my breast,
To hear from thy lattice breathed
The word that shall give me rest.
Open the door of thy heart,
And open thy chamber door,
And my kisses shall teach thy lips
The love that shall fade no more
    Till the sun grows cold,
    And the stars are old,
    And the leaves of the Judgment Book unfold.

SAUL

ROBERT BROWNING

Saul is one of the great narrative poems—the story of the shepherd boy David's rescue and healing of his King Saul, from a mood of black despair, by his song and his harp. Only a few verses are given here as a sample. Find the whole poem and discover it for yourself.

*   *   *

Then I tuned my harp, took off the lilies we twine round its
    chords
Lest they snap 'neath the stress of the noon-tide—those sun-
    beams like swords.
And I first played the tune all our sheep know, as, one after
    one,
So docile they come to the pen door till folding be done.
They are white and untorn by the bushes, for, lo, they have
    fed
Where the long grasses stifle the water within the stream's
    bed;
And now one after one seeks its lodging, as star follows star
Into eve and the blue far above us, so blue and so far.

Then the tune for which quails on the cornland will each
    leave his mate
To fly after the player; then, what makes the crickets elate
Till for boldness they fight one another; and then, what has
    weight
To set the quick jerboa a-musing outside his sand house—
There are none such as he for a wonder, half bird and half
    mouse.
God made all the creatures and gave them our love and our
    fear,
To give sign, we and they are his children, one family here.

Then I played the help-tune of our reapers, their wine-song,
    when hand
Grasps at hand, eye lights eye in good friendship, and great
    hearts expand
And grow one in the sense of this world's life. And then, the
    last song
When the dead man is praised on his journey, "Bear, bear
    him along,
With his few faults shut up like dead flowerets. Are balm-
    seeds not here
To console us? The land has none left such as he on the bier.
Oh, would we might keep thee, my brother!" And then, the
    glad chaunt
Of the marriage, first go the young maidens, next, she whom
    we vaunt
As the beauty, the pride, of our dwelling. And then, the great
    march
Wherein man runs to man to assist him and buttress an arch
Naught can break; who shall harm them, our friends? Then,
    the chorus intoned
As the Levites go up to the altar in glory enthroned.
But I stopped here: for here in the darkness Saul groaned.

And I paused, held my breath, in such silence, and listened
    apart
And the tent shook, for mighty Saul shuddered; and sparkles
    'gan dart
From the jewels that woke in his turban, at once with a start,
All its lordly male-sapphires, and rubies courageous at heart.
So the head; but the body still moved not, still hung there
    erect.
And I bent once again to my playing, pursued it unchecked.
As I sang;—

    "Oh, our manhood's prime vigor! No spirit feels waste,
Not a muscle is stopped in its playing nor sinew unbraced.

Oh, the wild joys of living! The leaping from rock up to
  rock,
The strong rending of boughs from the fir tree. The cool,
  silver shock
Of the plunge in the pool's living water, the hunt of the bear,
And the sultriness showing the lion is couched in his lair.
And the meal, the rich dates yellowed over with gold dust
  divine,
And the locust flesh steeped in the pitcher, the full draught
  of wine,
And the sleep in the dried river-channel where bulrushes tell
That the water was wont to go warbling so softly and well.
How good is man's life, the mere living! how fit to employ
All the heart and the soul and the senses forever in joy!"

    .   .   .   .

        Then fancies grew rife
Which had come long ago on the pasture, when round me
  the sheep
Fed in silence—above, the one eagle wheeled slow as in
  sleep;
And I lay in my hollow and mused on the world that might
  lie
'Neath his ken, though I saw but the strip 'twixt the hill and
  the sky;
And I laughed—"Since my days are ordained to be passed
  with my flocks,
Let me people at least, with my fancies, the plains and the
  rocks;
Dream the life I am never to mix with, and image the show
Of mankind as they live in those fashions I hardly shall
  know!
Schemes of life, its best rules and right uses, the courage that
  gains,
And the prudence that keeps what men strive for." And now
  these old trains

Of vague thought came again; I grew surer; so, once more the string
Of my harp made response to my spirit,

.　　.　　.　　.

Then first I was 'ware
That he sat, as I say, with my head just above his vast knees
Which were thrust out on each side around me, like oak-roots which please
To encircle a lamb when it slumbers. I looked up to know
If the best I could do had brought solace; he spoke not, but slow
Lifted up the hand slack at his side, till he laid it with care
Soft and grave, but in mild settled will, on my brow; through my hair
The large fingers were pushed, and he bent back my head with kind power—
All my face back, intent to peruse it, as men do a flower.
Thus held he me there with his great eyes that scrutinized mine—
And oh, all my heart, how it loved him! but where was the sign?
I yearned, "Could I help thee, my father, inventing a bliss,
I would add, to that life of the past, both the future and this;
I would give thee new life altogether, as good, ages hence,
As this moment, had love but the warrant, love's heart to dispense!"

.　　.　　.　　.

MORTE D'ARTHUR

ALFRED TENNYSON

*Morte d'Arthur is a part of "The Passing of Arthur," the last of
Tennyson's "Idylls of the King."*

So all day long the noise of battle roll'd
Among the mountains by the winter sea;
Until King Arthur's table, man by man,
Had fall'n in Lyonness about their Lord,
King Arthur: then, because his wound was deep,
The bold Sir Bedivere uplifted him,
Sir Bedivere, the last of all his knights,
And bore him to a chapel nigh the field,
A broken chancel with a broken cross,
That stood on a dark strait of barren land.
On one side lay the Ocean, and on one
Lay a great water, and the moon was full.

Then spake King Arthur to Sir Bedivere:
"The sequel of to-day unsolders all
The goodliest fellowship of famous knights
Whereof this world holds record. Such a sleep
They sleep—the men I loved. I think that we
Shall never more, at any future time,
Delight our souls with talk of knightly deeds,
Walking about the gardens and the halls
Of Camelot, as in the days that were.
I perish by this people which I made,—
Tho' Merlin sware that I should come again
To rule once more—but let what will be, be,
I am so deeply smitten thro' the helm
That without help I cannot last till morn.
Thou therefore take my brand Excalibur,
Which was my pride: for thou rememberest how

In those old days, one summer noon, an arm
Rose up from out the bosom of the lake,
Clothed in white samite, mystic, wonderful,
Holding the sword—and how I row'd across
And took it, and have worn it, like a king:
And, wheresoever I am sung or told
In aftertime, this also shall be known:
But now delay not: take Excalibur,
And fling him far into the middle mere:
Watch what thou seëst, and lightly bring me word."

    To him replied the bold Sir Bedivere:
"It is not meet, Sir King, to leave thee thus,
Aidless, alone, and smitten thro' the helm.
A little thing may harm a wounded man.
Yet I thy hest will all perform at full,
Watch what I see, and lightly bring thee word."
    So saying, from the ruin'd shrine he stept
And in the moon athwart the place of tombs,
Where lay the mighty bones of ancient men,
Old knights, and over them the sea-wind sang
Shrill, chill, with flakes of foam. He, stepping down
By zig-zag paths, and juts of pointed rock,
Came on the shining levels of the lake.
    There drew he forth the brand Excalibur,
And o'er him, drawing it, the winter moon,
Brightening the skirts of a long cloud, ran forth
And sparkled keen with frost against the hilt:
For all the haft twinkled with diamond sparks,
Myriads of topaz-lights, and jacinth-work
Of subtlest jewellery. He gazed so long
That both his eyes were dazzled, as he stood,
This way and that dividing the swift mind,
In act to throw: but at the last it seem'd
Better to leave Excalibur conceal'd

There in the many-knotted waterflags,
That whistled stiff and dry about the marge.
So strode he back slow to the wounded King.

Then spake King Arthur to Sir Bedivere:
"Hast thou perform'd my mission which I gave?
What is it thou hast seen? or what hast heard?"
    And answer made the bold Sir Bedivere:
"I heard the ripple washing in the reeds,
And the wild water lapping on the crag."
    To whom replied King Arthur, faint and pale:
"Thou hast betray'd thy nature and thy name,
Not rendering true answer, as beseem'd
Thy fëalty, nor like a noble knight:
For surer sign had follow'd, either hand,
Or voice, or else a motion of the mere.
This is a shameful thing for men to lie.
Yet now I charge thee, quickly go again
As thou art lief and dear, and do the thing
I bade thee, watch, and lightly bring me word."

    Then went Sir Bedivere the second time
Across the ridge, and paced beside the mere,
Counting the dewy pebbles, fix'd in thought;
But when he saw the wonder of the hilt,
How curiously and strangely chased, he smote
His palms together, and he cried aloud:

    "And if indeed I cast the brand away,
Surely a precious thing, one worthy note,
Should thus be lost for ever from the earth,
Which might have pleased the eyes of many men.
What good should follow this, if this were done?
What harm, undone? Deep harm to disobey,
Seeing obedience is the bond of rule.

Were it well to obey then, if a king demand
An act unprofitable, against himself?
The King is sick, and knows not what he does.
What record, or what relic of my lord
Should be to aftertime, but empty breath
And rumors of a doubt? But were this kept,
Stored in some treasure-house of mighty kings,
Some one might show it at a joust of arms,
Saying, 'King Arthur's sword, Excalibur,
Wrought by the lonely maiden of the Lake.
Nine years she wrought it, sitting in the deeps
Upon the hidden bases of the hills.'
So might some old man speak in the aftertime
To all the people, winning reverence.
But now much honor and much fame were lost."

So spake he, clouded with his own conceit,
And hid Excalibur the second time,
And so strode back slow to the wounded King.

Then spoke King Arthur, breathing heavily:
"What is it thou hast seen? or what hast heard?"

And answer made the bold Sir Bedivere:
"I heard the water lapping on the crag,
And the long ripple washing in the reeds."

To whom replied King Arthur, much in wrath:
"Ah, miserable and unkind, untrue,
Unknightly, traitor-hearted! Woe is me!
Authority forgets a dying king,
Laid widow'd of the power in his eye
That bow'd the will. I see thee what thou art,
For thou, the latest-left of all my knights
In whom should meet the offices of all,
Thou wouldst betray me for the precious hilt;

Either from lust of gold, or like a girl
Valuing the giddy pleasure of the eyes.
Yet, for a man may fail in duty twice,
And the third time may prosper, get thee hence:
But, if thou spare to fling Excalibur,
I will arise and slay thee with my hands."

Then quickly rose Sir Bedivere, and ran,
And, leaping down the ridges lightly, plunged
Among the bulrush-beds, and clutch'd the sword,
And strongly wheel'd and threw it. The great brand
Made lightnings in the splendor of the moon,
And flashing round and round, and whirl'd in an arch,
Shot like a streamer of the northern morn,
Seen where the moving isles of winter shock
By night, with noises of the northern sea.
So flash'd and fell the brand Excalibur:
But ere he dipt the surface, rose an arm
Clothed in white samite, mystic, wonderful,
And caught him by the hilt, and brandish'd him
Three times, and drew him under in the mere.
And lightly went the other to the King.

Then spoke King Arthur, drawing thicker breath:
"Now see I by thine eyes that this is done.
Speak out: what is it thou hast heard, or seen?"
And answer made the bold Sir Bedivere:
"Sir King, I closed mine eyelids, lest the gems
Should blind my purpose, for I never saw,
Nor shall see, here or elsewhere, till I die,
Not tho' I live three lives of mortal men,
So great a miracle as yonder hilt,
Then with both hands I flung him, wheeling him;
But when I look'd again, behold an arm,
Clothed in white samite, mystic, wonderful,

[83]

That caught him by the hilt, and brandish'd him
Three times, and drew him under in the mere."

    And answer made King Arthur, breathing hard:
"My end draws nigh; 'tis time that I were gone.
Make broad thy shoulders to receive my weight,
And bear me to the margin; yet I fear
My wound hath taken cold, and I shall die."
    So saying, from the pavement he half rose,
Slowly, with pain, reclining on his arm,
And looking wistfully with wide blue eyes
As in a picture. Him Sir Bedivere
Remorsefully regarded thro' his tears,
And would have spoken, but he found not words,
Then took with care, and kneeling on one knee,
O'er both his shoulders drew the languid hands,
And rising bore him thro' the place of tombs.
But, as he walk'd, King Arthur panted hard,
Like one that feels a nightmare on his bed
When all the house is mute. So sigh'd the King,
Muttering and murmuring at his ear, "Quick, quick!
I fear it is too late, and I shall die."
But the other swiftly strode from ridge to ridge,
Clothed with his breath, and looking, as he walk'd,
Larger than human on the frozen hills.
He heard the deep behind him, and a cry
Before. His own thought drove him like a goad.
Dry clash'd his harness in the icy caves
And barren chasms, and all to left and right
The bare black cliff clang'd round him, as he based
His feet on juts of slippery crag that rang
Sharp-smitten with the dint of armed heels—
And on a sudden, lo! the level lake,
And the long glories of the winter moon.
Then saw they how there hove a dusky barge

Dark as a funeral scarf from stem to stern,
Beneath them; and descending they were 'ware
That all the decks were dense with stately forms
Black-soled, black-hooded, like a dream—by these
Three Queens with crowns of gold—and from them rose
A cry that shiver'd to the tingling stars,
And, as it were one voice, an agony
Of lamentation, like a wind, that shrills
All night in a waste land, where no one comes,
Or hath come, since the making of the world.

Then murmur'd Arthur. "Place me in the barge."
And to the barge they came. There those three Queens
Put forth their hands, and took the King, and wept.
But she, that rose the tallest of them all
And fairest, laid his head upon her lap,
And loosed the shatter'd casque, and chafed his hands,
And call'd him by his name, complaining loud,
And dropping bitter tears against his brow
Striped with dark blood; for all his face was white
And colorless, and like the wither'd moon
Smote by the fresh beam of the springing east;
And all his greaves and cuisses dash'd with drops
Of onset; and the light and lustrous curls—
That made his forehead like a rising sun
High from the daïs-throne—were parch'd with dust;
Or, clotted into points and hanging loose,
Mix'd with the knightly growth that fringed his lips.
So like a shatter'd column lay the King;
Not like that Arthur who, with lance in rest,
From spur to plume a star of tournament,
Shot thro' the lists at Camelot, and charged
Before the eyes of ladies and of kings.

Then loudly cried the bold Sir Bedivere:

"Ah! My Lord Arthur, whither shall I go?
Where shall I hide my forehead and my eyes?
For now I see the true old times are dead,
When every morning brought a noble chance,
And every chance brought out a noble knight.
Such times have been not since the light that led
The holy Elders with the gift of myrrh.
But now the whole ROUND TABLE is dissolved
Which was an image of the mighty world;
And I, the last, go forth companionless,
And the days darken round me, and the years,
Among new men, strange faces, other minds."

And slowly answered Arthur from the barge:
"The old order changeth, yielding place to new,
And God fulfils himself in many ways,
Lest one good custom should corrupt the world.
Comfort thyself: what comfort is in me?
I have lived my life, and that which I have done
May He within himself make pure! but thou,
If thou shouldst never see my face again,
Pray for my soul. More things are wrought by prayer
Than this world dreams of. Wherefore, let thy voice
Rise like a fountain for me night and day.
For what are men better than sheep or goats
That nourish a blind life within the brain,
If, knowing God, they lift not hands of prayer
Both for themselves and those who call them friend?
For so the whole round earth is every way
Bound by gold chains about the feet of God.
But now farewell, I am going a long way
With these thou seëst—if indeed I go—
(For all my mind is clouded with a doubt)
To the island-valley of Avilion;
Where falls not hail, or rain, or any snow,

Nor ever wind blows loudly; but it lies
Deep-meadow'd, happy, fair with orchard-lawns
And bowery hollows crown'd with summer sea,
Where I will heal me of my grievous wound."

SIMON THE CYRENIAN SPEAKS

COUNTEE CULLEN

He never spoke a word to me,
And yet He called my name.
He never gave a sign to see,
And yet I knew and came.

At first I said, "I will not bear
His cross upon my back—
He only seeks to place it there
Because my skin is black."

But He was dying for a dream,
And He was very meek;
And in His eyes there shone a gleam
Men journey far to seek.

It was Himself my pity bought;
I did for Christ alone
What all of Rome could not have wrought
With bruise of lash or stone.

COLUMBUS

JOAQUIN MILLER

Behind him lay the gray Azores,
  Behind the Gates of Hercules;
Before him not the ghost of shores,
  Before him only shoreless seas.
The good mate said: "Now must we pray,
  For lo! the very stars are gone.
Brave Adm'r'l, speak; what shall I say?"
  "Why, say: 'Sail on! sail on! and on!' "

"My men grow mutinous day by day;
  My men grow ghastly wan and weak."
The stout mate thought of home; a spray
  Of salt wave washed his swarthy cheek.
"What shall I say, brave Adm'r'l, say,
  If we sight naught but seas at dawn?"
"Why, you shall say, at break of day:
  'Sail on! sail on! sail on! and on!' "

They sailed and sailed, as winds might blow,
  Until at last the blanched mate said:
"Why, now not even God would know
  Should I and all my men fall dead.
These very winds forget their way,
  For God from these dread seas is gone.
Now speak, brave Adm'r'l; speak and say"—
  He said: "Sail on! sail on! and on!"

They sailed. They sailed. Then spake the mate:
  "This mad sea shows his teeth to-night;
He curls his lips, he lies in wait,
  With lifted teeth, as if to bite:

Brave Adm'r'l, say but one good word;
    What shall we do when hope is gone?"
The words leapt like a leaping sword:
    "Sail on! sail on! sail on! and on!"

Then, pale and worn, he kept his deck,
    And peered through darkness. Ah, that night
Of all dark nights! And then a speck—
    A light! a light! a light! a light!
It grew, a starlit flag unfurled!
    It grew to be Time's burst of dawn.
He gained a world; he gave that world
    Its grandest lesson: "On! sail on!"

C. H. Miller was born November 10, 1841 in Indiana and as a boy of eleven journeyed farther westward by covered wagon. He wrote under the pen name of Joaquin Miller until his death in 1913.

SIMILAR CASES

CHARLOTTE PERKINS STETSON GILMAN

There was once a little animal,
    No bigger than a fox,
And on five toes he scampered
    Over Tertiary rocks
They called him Eohippus,
    And they called him very small,
And they thought him of no value—
    When they thought of him at all;
For the lumpish old Dinoceras
    And Coryphodon so slow
Were the heavy aristocracy
    In the days of long ago.

Said the little Eohippus,
  "I am going to be a horse!
And on my middle finger nails
  To run my earthly course!
I'm going to have a flowing tail!
  I'm going to have a mane!
I'm going to stand fourteen hands high
  On the psychozoic plane!"

The Coryphodon was horrified,
  The Dinoceras was shocked;
And they chased young Eohippus,
  But he skipped away and mocked.
Then they laughed enormous laughter,
  And they groaned enormous groans,
And they bade young Eohippus
  Go view his father's bones.

Said they, "You always were as small
  And mean as now we see,
And that's conclusive evidence
  That you're always going to be.
What! be a great, tall, handsome beast
  With hoofs to gallop on?
Why! You'd have to change your nature!"
  Said the Loxolophodon.
They considered him disposed of,
  And retired with gait serene;
That was the way they argued
  In the early Eocene.

There was once an Anthropoidal Ape,
  Far smarter than the rest,
And everything that they could do
  He always did the best;
So they naturally disliked him,
  And they gave him shoulders cool,

And when they had to mention him
    They said he was a fool.

Cried this pretentious Ape one day,
    "I'm going to be a Man!
And stand upright, and hunt, and fight,
    And conquer all I can!
I'm going to cut down forest trees,
    To make my houses higher!
I'm going to kill the Mastodon!
    I'm going to make a fire!"

Loud screamed the Anthropoidal Apes
    With laughter wild and gay;
They tried to catch that boastful one,
    But he always got away.
So they yelled at him in chorus,
    Which he minded not a whit;
And they pelted him with cocoanuts,
    Which didn't seem to hit.

And they gave him reasons
    Which they thought of much avail,
To prove how his preposterous
    Attempt was sure to fail.
Said the sages, "In the first place,
    The thing cannot be done!
And second, if it *could* be,
    It would not be any fun!

And third, and most conclusive,
    And admitting no reply,
You would have to change your nature!
    We should like to see you try!"
They chuckled then triumphantly,
    These lean and hairy shapes,
For these things passed as arguments
    With the Anthropoidal Apes.

There was once a Neolithic Man,
    An enterprising wight,
Who made his chopping inplements
    Unusually bright.
Unusually clever he,
    Unusually brave,
And he drew delightful Mammoths
    On the borders of his cave.

To his Neolithic neighbors,
    Who were startled and surprised,
Said he, "My friends, in course of time,
    We shall be civilized!
We are going to live in cities!
    We are going to fight in wars!
We are going to eat three times a day
    Without the natural cause!

"We are going to turn life upside down
    About a thing called gold!
We are going to want the earth, and take
    As much as we can hold!
We are going to wear great piles of stuff
    Outside our proper skins!
We are going to have Diseases!
    And Accomplishments!! and Sins!!!"

Then they all rose up in fury
    Against their boastful friend,
For prehistoric patience
    Cometh quickly to an end.
Said one, "This is chimerical!
    Utopian! Absurd!"
Said another, "What a stupid life!
    Too dull, upon my word!"

Cried all, "Before such things can come,
   You idiotic child,
You must alter Human Nature!"
   And they all sat back and smiled.
Thought they, "An answer to that last
   It will be hard to find!"
It was a clinching argument
   To the Neolithic Mind.

LINES FROM "SNOWBOUND"

JOHN GREENLEAF WHITTIER

When Whittier was a boy on his father's New England farm he had few books. One day he got hold of a battered copy of Burns' "Cotter's Saturday Night," which became his great treasure. He read and reread it. "Snowbound," written in 1866, about forty years later, is a sort of American "Cotter's Saturday Night." It is loved by readers everywhere as the best picture of a real old-fashioned New England winter that has ever been given in poetry.

The sun that brief December day
Rose cheerless over hills of gray,
And, darkly circled, gave at noon
A sadder light than waning moon.
Slow tracing down the thickening sky
Its mute and ominous prophecy,
A portent seeming less than threat,
It sank from sight before it set.
A chill no coat, however stout,
Of homespun stuff could quite shut out,
A hard, dull bitterness of cold,
That checked, mid-vein, the circling race
Of life-blood in the sharpened face,

The coming of the snow-storm told.
The wind blew east: we heard the roar
Of Ocean on his wintry shore,
And felt the strong pulse throbbing there
Beat with low rhythm our inland air.

Meanwhile we did our nightly chores,—
Brought in the wood from out of doors,
Littered the stalls, and from the mows
Raked down the herd's-grass for the cows;
Heard the horse whinnying for his corn;
And, sharply clashing horn on horn,
Impatient down the stanchion rows
The cattle shake their walnut bows;
While, peering from his early perch
Upon the scaffold's pole of birch,
The cock his crested helmet bent
And down his querulous challenge sent.

Unwarmed by any sunset light
The gray day darkened into night,
A night made hoary with the swarm
And whirlwind of the blinding storm,
As zigzag, wavering to and fro,
Crossed and re-crossed the wingèd snow.
And ere the early bed-time came
The white drift piled the window frame,
And through the dark the clothes-line posts
Looked in like tall and sheeted ghosts.

So all night long the storm roared on;
The morning broke without a sun;
In tiny spherule traced with lines
Of Nature's geometric signs,
In starry flake, and pellicle,

All day the hoary meteor fell;
And when the second morning shone,
We looked upon a world unknown,
On nothing we could call our own.
Around the glistening wonder bent
The blue walls of the firmament,
No clouds above, no earth below,—
A universe of sky and snow!
The old familiar sights of ours
Took marvellous shapes; strange domes **and towers**
Rose up where sty or corn-crib stood,
Or garden wall, or belt of wood;
A smooth white mound the brush pile showed,
A fenceless drift what once was road;
The bridle-post an old man sat
With loose-flung coat and high cocked hat;
The well-curb had a Chinese roof;
And even the long sweep, high aloof,
In its slant splendor, seemed to tell
Of Pisa's leaning miracle.

. . . .

Shut in from all the world without,
We sat the clean-winged hearth about,
Content to let the north wind roar
In baffled rage at pane and door,
While the red logs before us beat
The frost-line back with tropic heat;
And ever, when a louder blast
Shook beam and rafter as it passed,
The merrier up its roaring draught
The great throat of the chimney laughed.
The house-dog on his paws outspread
Laid to the fire his drowsy head,
The cat's dark silhouette on the wall
A couchant tiger's seemed to fall;

And, for the winter fireside meet,
Between the andirons' straddling feet,
The mug of cider simmered slow,
The apples sputtered in a row,
And close at hand the basket stood
With nuts from brown October's wood.

THE BLIND MEN AND THE ELEPHANT

JOHN GODFREY SAXE   *A Hindoo Fable*

It was six men of Indostan
    To learning much inclined,
Who went to see the Elephant
    (Though all of them were blind)
That each by observation
    Might satisfy his mind.

The *First* approached the Elephant,
    And happening to fall
Against his broad and sturdy side,
    At once began to bawl:
"God bless me! but the Elephant
    Is very like a wall!"

The *Second,* feeling of the tusk,
    Cried, "Ho! what have we here
So very round and smooth and sharp?
    To me 'tis mighty clear
This wonder of an Elephant
    Is very like a spear!"

The *Third* approached the animal,
  And happening to take
The squirming trunk within his hands,
  Thus boldly up and spake:
"I see," quoth he, "the Elephant
  Is very like a snake!"

The *Fourth* reached out an eager hand,
  And felt about the knee.
"What most this wondrous beast is like
  Is mighty plain," quoth he;
" 'Tis clear enough the Elephant
  Is very like a tree!"

The *Fifth* who chanced to touch the ear,
  Said: "E'en the blindest man
Can tell what this resembles most;
  Deny the fact who can,
This marvel of an Elephant
  Is very like a fan!"

The *Sixth* no sooner had begun
  About the beast to grope,
Than, seizing on the swinging tail
  That fell within his scope,
"I see," quoth he, "the Elephant
  Is very like a rope!"

And so these men of Indostan
  Disputed loud and long,
Each in his own opinion
  Exceeding stiff and strong,
Though each was partly in the right,
  And all were in the wrong!

The Moral:

So oft in theologic wars,
　　The disputants, I ween,
Rail on in utter ignorance
　　Of what each other mean,
　And prate about an Elephant
　Not one of them has seen!

WIDDICOMBE FAIR

Traditional: English

Tom Pearse, Tom Pearse, lend me your gray mare,
　All along, down along, out along, lee.
For I want to go to Widdicombe Fair,
　Wi' Bill Brewer, Jan Stewer, Peter Gurney, Peter Davy,
　Dan'l Whiddon, Harry Hawk,
Old Uncle Tom Cobleigh and all.'
　Old Uncle Tom Cobleigh and all.

'And when shall I see again my gray mare?'—
　All along, down along, out along, lee.
'By Friday soon, or Saturday noon,
　Wi' Bill Brewer, Jan Stewer, Peter Gurney, Peter Davy,
　Dan'l Whiddon, Harry Hawk,
Old Uncle Tom Cobleigh and all.
　Old Uncle Tom Cobleigh and all.

Then Friday came and Saturday noon,
　All along, down along, out along, lee.
But Tom Pearse's old mare hath not trotted home,
　Wi' Bill Brewer, Jan Stewer, Peter Gurney, Peter Davy,
　Dan'l Whiddon, Harry Hawk,

Old Uncle Tom Cobleigh and all.
  Old Uncle Tom Cobleigh and all.

So Tom Pearse he got up to the top o' the hill,
  All along, down along, out along, lee.
And he sees his old mare down a-making her will,
  Wi' Bill Brewer, Jan Stewer, Peter Gurney, Peter Davy,
  Dan'l Whiddon, Harry Hawk,
Old Uncle Tom Cobleigh and all.'
  Old Uncle Tom Cobleigh and all.

So Tom Pearse's old mare her took sick and her died,
  All along, down along, out along, lee.
And Tom he sat down on a stone, and he cried
  Wi' Bill Brewer, Jan Stewer, Peter Gurney, Peter Davy,
  Dan'l Whiddon, Harry Hawk,
Old Uncle Tom Cobleigh and all.
  Old Uncle Tom Cobleigh and all.

But this isn't the end o' this shocking affair,
  All along, down along, out along, lee.
Nor, though they be dead, of the horrid career
  Of Bill Brewer, Jan Stewer, Peter Gurney, Peter Davy,
  Dan'l Whiddon, Harry Hawk,
Old Uncle Tom Cobleigh and all.
  Old Uncle Tom Cobleigh and all.

When the wind whistles cold on the moor of a night,
  All along, down along, out along, lee.
Tom Pearse's old mare doth appear, gashly white,
  Wi' Bill Brewer, Jan Stewer, Peter Gurney, Peter Davy,
  Dan'l Whiddon, Harry Hawk,
Old Uncle Tom Cobleigh and all.
  Old Uncle Tom Cobleigh and all.

And all the long night be heard skirling and groans,
    All along, down along, out along, lee.
From Tom Pearse's old mare in her rattling bones,
    And from Bill Brewer, Jan Stewer, Peter Gurney, Peter
        Davy,
    Dan'l Whiddon, Harry Hawk,
Old Uncle Tom Cobleigh and all.
    OLD UNCLE TOM COBLEIGH AND ALL.

"FLASH:" THE FIREMAN'S STORY

WILL CARLETON

Flash was a white-foot sorrel, an' run on Number Three:
Not much stable manners—an average horse to see;
Notional in his methods—strong in loves an' hates;
Not very much respected, or popular 'mongst his mates.

Dull an' moody an' sleepy, an' "off" on quiet days;
Full o' turbulent, sour looks, an' small, sarcastic ways;
Scowled an' bit at his partner, and banged the stable
    floor—
With other means intended to designate life a bore.

But when, be 't day or night time he heard the alarm-bell ring,
He'd rush for his place in the harness with a regular tiger
    spring;
An' watch, with nervous shivers, the clasp of buckle an' band,
Until 'twas plainly evident he'd like to lend a hand.

An' when the word was given, away he would rush and tear,
As if a thousand witches was rumplin' up his hair,
An' craze the other horses with his magnetic charm,
Till every hoof-beat sounded a regular fire alarm!

Never a horse a jockey would notice and admire
Like Flash in front of his engine a-runnin' to a fire;
Never a horse so lazy, so dawdlin' an' so slack,
As Flash upon his return trip a-drawin' the engine back.

Now, when the different horses gets tender-footed an' old,
They're no use in our business; so Flash was finally sold
To quite a respectable milkman, who found it not so fine
A-bossin' one o' God's creatures outside its natural line.

Seems as if I could see Flash a-mopin' along here now,
Feelin' that he was simply assistant to a cow;
But sometimes he'd imagine he heard the alarm-bell's din
An' jump an' rear for a season before they could hold him in.

An' once, in spite o' his master, he strolled in 'mongst us
    chaps,
To talk with the other horses, of former fires, perhaps;
Whereat the milkman kicked him; whereat, us boys to please,
He begged that horse's pardon upon his bended knees.

But one day, for a big fire as we was makin' a dash,
Both o' the horses we had on somewhat resemblin' Flash,
Yellin' an' ringin' an' rushin', with excellent voice an' heart,
We passed the poor old fellow a-tuggin' away at his cart.

If ever I see an old hoss grow upward into a new—
If ever I see a milkman whose traps behind him flew,
'Twas that old hoss, a-rearin' an' racin' down the track,
An' that respectable milkman a-tryin' to hold him back.

Away he rushed like a cyclone for the head o' "Number
    Three,"
Gained the lead an' kept it, an' steered his journey free;
Dodgin' wagons an' horses, an' still on the keenest "silk,"

An' furnishin' all that neighborhood with good, respectable
   milk.

Crowd a-yellin' an' runnin', an' vainly hollerin' "Whoa!"
Milkman bracin' an' sawin', with never a bit o' show;
Firemen laughin' an' chucklin', an' shoutin' "Good! go in!"
Hoss a-gettin' down to it, an' sweepin' along like sin.

Finally came where the fire was—halted with a "thud";
Sent the respectable milkman heels over head in mud;
Watched till he see the engines properly workin' there,
After which he relinquished all interest in the affair.

Moped an' wilted an' dawdled, "faded away" once more,
Took up his old occupation—considerin' life a bore;
Laid down in his harness, an'—sorry I am to say—
The milkman he had drawn there took his dead body away.

That's the whole o' my story; I've seen, more'n once or twice,
That poor dead animal's actions is full o' human advice;
An' if you ask what Flash taught, I'll simply answer, then,
That poor old horse was a symbol of some intelligent men.

An' if, as some consider, there's animals in the sky,
I think the poor old fellow is gettin' another try;
But if he should sniff the big fire that plagues the abode o' sin,
It'll take the strongest angel to hold the old fellow in.

THE BRONCHO THAT WOULD NOT BE BROKEN

VACHEL LINDSAY

A little colt—broncho, loaned to the farm
To be broken in time without fury or harm,
Yet black crows flew past you, shouting alarm,
Calling "Beware," with lugubrious singing . . .
The butterflies there in the bush were romancing,
The smell of the grass caught your soul in a trance,
So why be a-fearing the spurs and the traces,
O broncho that would not be broken of dancing?

You were born with the pride of the lords great and olden
Who danced, through the ages, in corridors golden.
In all the wide farm-place the person most human.
You spoke out so plainly with squealing and capering,
With whinnying, snorting, contorting and prancing,
As you dodged your pursuers, looking askance,
With Greek-footed figures, and Parthenon paces,
O broncho that would not be broken of dancing.

The grasshoppers cheered. "Keep whirling," they said.
The insolent sparrows called from the shed
"If men will not laugh, make them wish they were dead."
But arch were your thoughts, all malice displacing.
Though the horse-killers came, with snake-whips advancing.
You bantered and cantered away your last chance.
And they scourged you, with Hell in their speech and their
   faces,
O broncho that would not be broken of dancing.

"Nobody cares for you," rattled the crows,
As you dragged the whole reaper, next day, down the rows.

The three mules held back, yet you danced on your toes.
You pulled like a racer, and kept the mules chasing.
You tangled the harness with bright eyes side-glancing,
While the drunk driver bled you—a pole for a lance—
And the giant mules bit at you—keeping their places.
O broncho that would not be broken of dancing.

In that last afternoon your boyish heart broke.
The hot wind came down like a sledge-hammer stroke.
The blood-sucking flies to a rare feast awoke.
And they searched out your wounds, your death-warrant
    tracing.
And the merciful men, their religion enhancing,
Stopped the red reaper, to give you a chance.
Then you died on the prairie, and scorned all disgraces,
O broncho that would not be broken of dancing.

UNDER THE GOAL POSTS

ARTHUR GUITERMAN

We had battered their weakening rush line till it gave like
    a wisp of grass
To the push of the padded shoulder and the brunt of the
    plunging mass.
And thrice, by our heavy rushes and runs that would stir your
    soul,
We had carried the grass-stained football in triumph beyond
    their goal.
Defeated, wearied, hopeless, five minutes more to play,
They lined beneath their goal posts—our dearest foes at
    bay.

Across the trampled oval there loomed a steady roar
That shook the crowded benches, demanding "One more
    score!"
Their plucky little quarter held up a muddy hand;
We heard his hearty whisper: "We'll hold 'em; now, boys,
    stand!"

We hurled our weight upon them; their center met the shock
Well-braced, with hip and shoulder, and held us like a rock.
Again we charged; they wavered, they bent and swayed—
    and then
They surged as ocean surges and bore us back again.
We tried for goal; our fullback drove the pigskin clear and
    fair;
Their sturdy guards came leaping through and blocked it in
    the air.
Each arm became a bulwark, each chest became a shield,
And steady as a phalanx they bucked us down the field
Until the last shrill whistle and banners wildly tossed
Proclaimed the game was over. We'd won, and they had lost.
They lost, yet half in triumph. 'Tis not that I would seem
To dim the cloudless glories of our great, unbeaten team,
But still, should fortune fail us at length, the hope is mine
That we may stand as they did upon the last white line;
That we may show the courage and stubbornness of soul
That balked our eager rushers beneath their very goal.

CASEY AT THE BAT

ERNEST LAWRENCE THAYER

It looked extremely rocky for the Mudville nine that day;
The score stood two to four, with but an inning left to play.
So, when Cooney died at second, and Burrows did the same,
A pallor wreathed the features of the patrons of the game.

A straggling few got up to go, leaving there the rest,
With that hope which springs eternal within the human
    breast.
For they thought: "If only Casey could get a whack at that,"
They'd put even money now, with Casey at the bat.

But Flynn preceded Casey, and likewise so did Blake,
And the former was a pudd'n, and the latter was a fake.
So on that stricken multitude a deathlike silence sat;
For there seemed but little chance of Casey's getting to the
    bat.

But Flynn let drive a "single," to the wonderment of all.
And the much-despised Blakey "tore the cover off the ball."
And when the dust had lifted, and they saw what had oc-
    curred,
There was Blakey safe at second, and Flynn a-huggin' third.

Then from the gladdened multitude went up a joyous
    yell—
It rumbled in the mountaintops, it rattled in the dell;
It struck upon the hillside and rebounded on the flat;
For Casey, mighty Casey, was advancing to the bat.

There was ease in Casey's manner as he stepped into his
    place,

There was pride in Casey's bearing and a smile on Casey's
    face;
And when responding to the cheers he lightly doffed his hat,
No stranger in the crowd could doubt 'twas Casey at the bat.

Ten thousand eyes were on him as he rubbed his hands with
    dirt,
Five thousand tongues applauded when he wiped them on his
    shirt;
Then when the writhing pitcher ground the ball into his hip,
Defiance glanced in Casey's eye, a sneer curled Casey's lip.

And now the leather-covered sphere came hurtling through
    the air,
And Casey stood a-watching it in haughty grandeur there.
Close by the sturdy batsman the ball unheeded sped;
"That ain't my style," said Casey. "Strike one," the umpire
    said.

From the benches, black with people, there went up a muffled
    roar,
Like the beating of the storm waves on the stern and distant
    shore.
"Kill him! kill the umpire!" shouted someone on the stand;
And it's likely they'd have killed him had not Casey raised
    his hand.

With a smile of Christian charity great Casey's visage shone;
He stilled the rising tumult, he made the game go on;
He signaled to the pitcher, and once more the spheroid
    flew;
But Casey still ignored it, and the umpire said, "Strike two."

"Fraud!" cried the maddened thousands, and the echo an-
    swered "Fraud!"

But one scornful look from Casey and the audience was
    awed;
They saw his face grow stern and cold, they saw his muscles
    strain,
And they knew that Casey wouldn't let the ball go by again.

The sneer is gone from Casey's lips, his teeth are clenched
    in hate,
He pounds with cruel vengeance his bat upon the plate;
And now the pitcher holds the ball, and now he lets it go,
And now the air is shattered by the force of Casey's blow.

Oh, somewhere in this favored land the sun is shining bright,
The band is playing somewhere, and somewhere hearts are
    light;
And somewhere men are laughing, and somewhere children
    shout,
But there is no joy in Mudville: Mighty Casey has struck out.

THE YARN OF THE *NANCY BELL*

WILLIAM S. GILBERT

'Twas on the shores that round our coast
From Deal to Ramsgate span,
That I found alone on a piece of stone
An elderly naval man.

His hair was weedy, his beard was long,
And weedy and long was he,
And I heard this wight on the shore recite,
In a singular minor key;

"Oh, I am a cook, and the captain bold,
And the mate of the *Nancy* brig,

And a bo'sun tight, and a midshipmite,
And the crew of the captain's gig!"

And he shook his fists and he tore his hair,
Till I really felt afraid,
For I couldn't help thinking the man had been drinking,
And so I simply said:

"Oh, elderly man, it's little I know
Of the duties of men of the sea,
But I'll eat my hand if I understand
How you can possibly be

"At once a cook, and a captain bold,
And the mate of the *Nancy* brig,
And a bo'sun tight, and a midshipmite,
And the crew of the captain's gig."

Then he gave a hitch to his trousers, which
Is a trick all seamen larn,
And having got rid of a thumping quid,
He spun this painful yarn:

" 'Twas in the good ship *Nancy Bell*
That we sailed to the Indian sea,
And there on a reef we came to grief,
Which has often occurred to me.

"And pretty nigh all o' the crew was drowned
(There was seventy-seven o' soul),
And only ten of the *Nancy's* men
Said 'Here' to the muster roll.

"There was me and the cook and the captain bold,
And the mate of the *Nancy* brig,

And the bo'sun tight, and a midshipmite,
And the crew of the captain's gig.

"For a month we'd neither wittles nor drink,
Till a-hungary we did feel,
So we drawed a lot, and accordin' shot
The captain for our meal.

"The next lot fell to the *Nancy's* mate,
And a delicate dish he made;
Then our appetite with the midshipmite
We seven survivors stayed.

"And then we murdered the bo'sun tight,
And he much resembled pig;
Then we wittled free, did the cook and me,
On the crew of the captain's gig.

"Then only the cook and me was left,
And the delicate question 'which
Of us two goes to the kettle?' arose
And we argued it out as sich.

"For I loved that cook as a brother, I did,
And the cook he worshipped me;
But we'd both be blowed if we'd either be stowed
In the other chap's hold, you see.

" 'I'll be eat if you dines off me,' says Tom,
'Yes, that,' says I, 'you'll be!'
'I'm boiled if I die, my friend,' quoth I,
And 'Exactly so!' quoth he.

"Says he, 'Dear James, to murder me
Were a foolish thing to do,

For don't you see that you can't cook me,
While I can—and will—cook you?'

"So he boils the water and takes the salt
And the pepper in portions true
(Which he never forgot), and some chopped shalot,
And some sage and parsley, too.

" 'Come here,' says he, with proper pride,
Which his smiling features tell,
' 'Twill soothing be if I let you see,
How extremely nice you'll smell.'

"And he stirred it round and round and round
And he sniffed at the foaming froth;
When I ups with his heels, and smothers his squeals
In the scum of the boiling broth.

"And I eat that cook in a week or less,
And—as I eating be
The last of his chops, why, I almost drops,
For a vessel in sight I see.

"And I never grieve, and I never smile,
And I never larf nor play
But I sit and croak, and a single joke
I have—which is to say;

"Oh, I am a cook, and a captain bold,
And the mate of the *Nancy* brig,
And a bo'sun tight, and a midshipmite,
And the crew of the captain's gig!"

Gilbert is the writer of many humorous ballads and light-opera librettos for which Arthur Sullivan wrote the music. This is one of his famous "Bab Ballads" and was the poem that started his great success in England.

JIM BLUDSO OF THE *PRAIRIE BELLE*

JOHN HAY

Wall, no! I can't tell whar he lives,
    Because he don't live, you see;
Leastways, he's got out of the habit
    Of livin' like you and me.
Whar have you been for the last three year
    That you haven't heard folks tell
How Jimmy Bludso passed in his checks
    The night of the *Prairie Belle?*

He wasn't no saint,—them engineers
    Is all pretty much alike,—
One wife in Natchez-under-the-Hill
    And another one here, in Pike;
A keerless man in his talk, was Jim,
    And an awkward hand in a row,
But he never flunked, and he never lied,—
    I reckon he never knowed how.

And this was all the religion he had,
    To treat his engine well;
Never be passed on the river;
    To mind the pilot's bell;
And if ever the *Prairie Belle* took fire,—
    A thousand times he swore
He'd hold her nozzle agin the bank
    Till the last soul got ashore.

All boats has their day on the Mississip,
    And her day come at last,—
The *Movastar* was a better boat,
    But the *Belle* she *wouldn't* be passed.

And so she come tearin' along that night—
    The oldest craft on the line—
With a nigger squat on her safety-valve,
    And her furnace crammed, rosin and pine.

The fire bust out as she cl'ared the bar,
    And burnt a hole in the night,
And quick as a flash she turned, and made
    For that willer-bank on the right.
There was runnin' and cursin', but Jim yelled out,
    Over all the infernal roar,
"I'll hold her nozzle agin the bank
    Till the last galoot's ashore."

Through the hot, black breath of the burnin' boat
    Jim Bludso's voice was heard,
And they all had trust in his cussedness,
    And knowed he would keep his word.
And, sure's you're born, they all got off
    Afore the smokestacks fell,—
And Bludso's ghost went up alone
    In the smoke of the *Prairie Belle*.

He weren't no saint,—but at jedgment
    I'd run my chance with Jim,
'Longside of some pious gentlemen
    That wouldn't shook hands with him.
He seen his duty, a dead-sure thing,—
    And went for it thar and then;
And Christ ain't a going to be too hard
    On a man that died for men.

John Hay, as a young man, studied law in Abraham Lincoln's Springfield office, and when Lincoln went to Washington as President, he offered Hay the position of private secretary, a post Hay held till Lincoln's death.

THE HEIGHT OF THE RIDICULOUS

OLIVER WENDELL HOLMES

I wrote some lines once on a time
　In wondrous merry mood,
And thought, as usual, men would say
　They were exceeding good.

They were so queer, so very queer,
　I laughed as I would die;
Albeit, in the general way,
　A sober man am I.

I called my servant, and he came;
　How kind it was of him
To mind a slender man like me,
　He of the mighty limb!

"These to the printer," I exclaimed,
　And, in my humorous way,
I added (as a trifling jest),
　"There'll be the devil to pay."

He took the paper, and I watched,
　And saw him peep within;
At the first line he read, his face
　Was all upon the grin.

He read the next; the grin grew broad,
　And shot from ear to ear;
He read the third; a chuckling noise
　I now began to hear.

The fourth; he broke into a roar;
　　The fifth; his waistband split;
The sixth; he burst five buttons off,
　　And tumbled in a fit.

Ten days and nights, with sleepless eye,
　　I watched that wretched man,
And since, I never dare to write
　　As funny as I can.

SNAKE

D. H. LAWRENCE

A snake came to my water-trough
On a hot, hot day, and I in pyjamas for the heat,
To drink there.

In the deep, strange-scented shade of the great dark carob-
　　tree
I came down the steps with my pitcher
And must wait, must stand and wait, for there he was at the
　　trough before me.
He reached down from a fissure in the earth-wall in the gloom
And trailed his yellow-brown slackness soft-bellied down,
　　over the edge of the stone trough
And rested his throat upon the stone bottom,
And where the water had dripped from the tap, in a small
　　clearness,
He sipped with his straight mouth,
Softly drank through his straight gums, into his slack long
　　body,
Silently.

Snake

Someone was before me at my water-trough,
And I, like a second comer, waiting.

He lifted his head from his drinking, as cattle do,
And looked at me vaguely, as drinking cattle do,
And flickered his two-forked tongue from his lips, and mused
    a moment,
And stooped and drank a little more,
Being earth brown, earth golden from the burning burning
    bowels of the earth
On the day of Sicilian July, with Etna smoking.

The voice of my education said to me
He must be killed,
For in Sicily the black, black snakes are innocent, the gold
    are venomous.

And voices in me said, If you were a man
You would take a stick and break him now, and finish him off.

But I must confess how I liked him,
How glad I was he had come like a guest in quiet, to drink
    at my water-trough
And depart peaceful, pacified, and thankless,
Into the burning bowels of this earth.

Was it cowardice, that I dared not kill him?
Was it perversity, that I longed to talk to him?
Was it humility, to feel so honoured?
I felt so honoured.

And yet those voices:
If you were not afraid, you would kill him!

And truly I was afraid, I was most afraid,
But even so, honoured still more
That he should seek my hospitality
From out the dark door of the secret earth.

He drank enough
And lifted his head, dreamily, as one who has drunken,
And flickered his tongue like a forked night on the air, so
    black,
Seeming to lick his lips,
And looked around like a god, unseeing, into the air,
And slowly turned his head,
And slowly, very slowly, as if thrice adream,
Proceeded to draw his slow length curving round
And climb again the broken bank of my wall-face.

And as he put his head into that dreadful hole,
And as he slowly drew up, snake-easing his shoulders, and
    entered farther,
A sort of horror, a sort of protest against his withdrawing
    into that horrid black hole,
Deliberately going into the blackness, and slowly drawing
    himself after,
Overcame me now his back was turned.
I looked round, I put down my pitcher,
I picked up a clumsy log
And threw it at the water-trough with a clatter.

I think it did not hit him,
But suddenly that part of him that was left behind convulsed
    in undignified haste,
Writhed like lightning, and was gone
Into the black hole, the earth-lipped fissure in the wall-front,
At which, in the intense still noon, I stared with fascination.

Snake

And immediately I regretted it.
I thought how paltry, how vulgar, what a mean act!
I despised myself and the voices of my accursed human education.

And I thought of the albatross,
And I wished he would come back, my snake.

For he seemed to me again like a king,
Like a king in exile, uncrowned in the underworld,
Now due to be crowned again.

And so, I missed my chance with one of the lords
Of life.
And I have something to expiate:
A pettiness.

THE RUNAWAY

ROBERT FROST

Once, when the snow of the year was beginning to fall,
We stopped by a mountain pasture to say "Whose colt?"
A little Morgan had one forefoot on the wall,
The other curled at his breast. He dipped his head
And snorted at us. And then he had to bolt.
We heard the miniature thunder where he fled
And we saw him, or thought we saw him, dim and grey,
Like a shadow against the curtain of falling flakes.
"I think the little fellow's afraid of the snow.
He isn't winter-broken. It isn't play
With the little fellow at all. He's running away.
I doubt if even his mother could tell him, 'Sakes,
It's only weather.' He'd think she didn't know!

Where is his mother? He can't be out alone."
And now he comes again with a clatter of stone
And mounts the wall again with whited eyes
And all his tail that isn't hair up straight.
He shudders his coat as if to throw off flies.
"Whoever it is that leaves him out so late,
When other creatures have gone to stall and bin,
Ought to be told to come and take him in."

LITTLE LOST PUP

ARTHUR GUITERMAN

He was lost!—not a shade of doubt of that;
For he never barked at a slinking cat,
But stood in the square where the wind blew raw
With a drooping ear and a trembling paw
And a mournful look in his pleading eye
And a plaintive sniff at the passer-by
That begged as plain as a tongue could sue,
"O Mister! please may I follow you?"
A lorn wee waif of a tawny brown
Adrift in the roar of a heedless town.
Oh, the saddest of sights in a world of sin
Is a little lost pup with his tail tucked in!

Now he shares my board and he owns my bed,
And he fairly shouts when he hears my tread;
Then, if things go wrong, as they sometimes do,
He asserts his right to assuage my woes
With a warm, red tongue and a nice, cold nose
And a silky head on my arm or knee
And a paw as soft as a paw can be.

When we rove the woods for a league about
He's as full of pranks as a school let out;
For he romps and frisks like a three months' colt,
And he runs me down like a thunderbolt.
Oh, the blithest of sights in the world so fair
Is a gay little pup with his tail in the air!

THE HORSE THIEF

WILLIAM ROSE BENÉT

There he moved, cropping the grass at the purple canyon's
    lip.
    His mane was mixed with the moonlight that silvered his
        snow-white side,
For the moon sailed out of a cloud with the wake of a spectral
    ship,
    I crouched and I crawled on my belly, my lariat coil looped
        wide.

Dimly and dark the mesas broke on the starry sky.
    A pall covered every color of their gorgeous glory at noon.
I smelt the yucca and mesquite, and stifled my heart's quick
    cry,
    And wormed and crawled on my belly to where he moved
        against the moon!

Some Moorish barb was that mustang's sire. His lines were
    beyond all wonder.
    From the prick of his ears to the flow of his tail he ached
       in my throat and eyes.
Steel and velvet grace! As the prophet says, God had
    "clothed his neck with thunder."

Oh, marvelous with the drifting cloud he drifted across the skies!

And then I was near at hand—crouched, and balanced, and cast the coil;
And the moon was smothered in cloud, and the rope through my hands with a rip!
But somehow I gripped and clung, with the blood in my brain aboil—
With a turn round the rugged tree-stump there on the purple canyon's lip.

Right into the stars he reared aloft, his red eye rolling and raging.
He whirled and sunfished and lashed, and rocked the earth to thunder and flame.
He squealed like a regular devil horse. I was haggard and spent and aging—
Roped clean, but almost storming clear, his fury too fierce to tame.

And I cursed myself for a tenderfoot moon-dazzled to play the part,
But I was doubly desperate then, with the posse pulled out from town,
Or I'd never have tried it. I only knew I must get a mount and a start.
The filly had snapped her foreleg short. I had had to shoot her down.

So there he struggled and strangled, and I snubbed him around the tree.
Nearer, a little nearer—hoofs planted, and lolling tongue—

Till a sudden slack pitched me backward. He reared right on
    top of me.
    Mother of God—that moment! He missed me . . . and
      up I swung.

Somehow, gone daft completely and clawing a bunch of his
    mane,
    As he stumbled and tripped in the lariat, there I was—up
      and astride
And cursing for seven counties! And the mustang? *Just in-
sane!*
    Crack-bang! went the rope; we cannoned off the tree—
      then—gods, that ride!

A rocket—that's all, a rocket! I dug with my teeth and nails.
    Why we never hit even the high spots (though I hardly
      remember things,)
But I heard a monstrous booming like a thunder of flapping
    sails
    When he spread—well, *call* me a liar!—when he spread
      those wings, those wings!

So white that my eyes were blinded, thick-feathered and wide
    unfurled,
    They beat the air into billows. We sailed, and the earth
      was gone.
Canyon and desert and mesa withered below, with the world.
    And then I knew that mustang; for I—was Bellerophon!

Yes, glad as the Greek, and mounted on a horse of the elder
    gods,
    With never a magic bridle or a fountain-mirror night!
My chaps and spurs and holster must have looked it? What's
    the odds?

I'd a leg over lightning and thunder, careering across the
sky!

And forever streaming before me, fanning my forehead cool,
Flowed a mane of molten silver; and just before my
thighs
(As I gripped his velvet-muscled ribs, which I cursed myself
for a fool)
The steady pulse of those pinions—their wonderful fall
and rise!

The bandanna I bought in Bowie blew loose and whipped
from my neck.
My shirt was stuck to my shoulders and ribboning out
behind.
The stars were dancing, wheeling and glancing, dipping with
smirk and beck.
The clouds were flowing, dusking and glowing. We rode
a roaring wind.

We soared through the silver starlight to knock at the
planets' gates.
New shimmering constellations came whirling into our
ken.
Red stars and green and golden swung out of the void that
waits
For man's great last adventure; the Signs took shape—
and then

I knew the lines of that Centaur the moment I saw him come!
The musical-box of the heavens all around us rolled to a
tune
That tinkled and chimed and trilled with silver sounds that
struck you dumb,

As if some archangel were grinding out the music of the
 moon.

Melody-drunk on the Milky Way, as we swept and soared
 hilarious,
  Full in our pathway, sudden he stood—the Centaur of the
   Stars,
 Flashing from head and hoofs and breast! I knew him for
  Sagittarius.
  He reared, and bent and drew his bow. He crouched as a
   boxer spars.

Flung back on his haunches, weird he loomed—then leapt—
 and the dim void lightened.
  Old White Wings shied and swerved aside, and fled from
   the splendor-shod.
 Through a flashing welter of worlds we charged. I knew why
  my horse was frightened.
  He *had* two faces—a dog's and a man's—that Babylonian
   god!

Also, he followed us real as fear. Ping! went an arrow past.
  My broncho buck-jumped, humping high. We plunged
   . . . I guess that's all!
 I lay on the purple canyon's lip, when I opened my eyes at
  last—
  Stiff and sore and my head like a drum, but I broke no
   bones in the fall.

So you know—and now you may string me up. Such was the
 way you caught me.
  Thank you for letting me tell it straight, though you never
   could greatly care.
 For I took a horse that wasn't mine! . . . But there's one
  the heavens brought me,

And I'll hang right happy, because I know he is waiting
    for me up there.

From creamy muzzle to cannon-bone, by God, he's a peerless
    wonder!
He is steel and velvet and furnace-fire, and death's su-
    premest prize;
And never again shall be roped on earth that neck that is
    "clothed with thunder" . . .
String me up, Dave! Go dig my grave! *I rode him across*
    the skies!

Part Two

OUTDOOR POEMS

Life is sweet, brother . . .
There's day and night, brother, both sweet things;
Sun, moon and stars, brother, all sweet things;
There's likewise a wind on the heath.

George Borrow in *Lavengro*

SPRING

RICHARD HOVEY

I said in my heart, "I am sick of four walls and a ceiling.
I have need of the sky.
I have business with the grass.
I will up and get me away where the hawk is wheeling,
Lone and high,
And the slow clouds go by. . . ."

LINES WRITTEN ABOVE TINTERN ABBEY

WILLIAM WORDSWORTH

For I have learned
To look on Nature, not as in the hour
Of thoughtless youth; but hearing oftentimes
The still, sad music of humanity,
Not harsh nor grating, though of ample power
To chasten and subdue. And I have felt
A presence that disturbs me with the joy
Of elevated thoughts; a sense sublime
Of something far more deeply interfused,
Whose dwelling is the light of setting suns,
And the round ocean and the living air,
And the blue sky and in the mind of man:
A motion and a spirit that impels
All thinking things, all objects of all thought,
And rolls through all things. Therefore am I still
A lover of the meadows and the woods,
And mountains; and of all that we behold
From this green earth; of all the mighty world

Of eye and ear, both what they half create,
And what perceive; well pleased to recognize
In nature and the language of the sense,
The anchor of my purest thoughts, the nurse,
The guide, the guardian of my heart, and soul
Of all my moral being.

William Wordsworth is one of the firm pillars of English poetry. In 1798 he and Samuel T. Coleridge (the man who wrote "The Rime of the Ancient Mariner"), believing that good poetry could be written about the humble, everyday people as well as about kings and warriors, published a book of poems called "Lyrical Ballads" to prove it. Most of Wordsworth's poems are about nature.

CAMPER'S NIGHT SONG

ROBERT LOUIS STEVENSON

The bed was made, the room was fit,
By punctual eve the stars were lit;
The air was sweet, the water ran;
No need was there for maid or man,
When we put up, my ass and I,
At God's green caravanserai.

THE VAGABOND

ROBERT LOUIS STEVENSON

Give to me the life I love,
  Let the lave go by me,
Give the jolly heaven above
  And the byway nigh me.
Bed in the bush with stars to see,
  Bread I dip in the river—

There's the life for a man like me,
    There's the life for ever.

Or let autumn fall on me
    Where afield I linger,
Silencing the bird on tree,
    Biting the blue finger.
White as meal the frosty field—
    Warm the fireside haven—
Not to autumn will I yield,
    Not to winter even!

Let the blow fall soon or late,
    Let what will be o'er me;
Give the face of earth around,
    And the road before me,
Wealth I ask not, hope nor love,
    Nor a friend to know me;
All I ask, the heaven above
    And the road below me.

Gallant, courageous Robert Louis Stevenson, in his life-long fight for health, learned well the joys of the open road. He tells the story of his vagabond days in "Travels With a Donkey" and "The Inland Voyage."

THE COROMANDEL FISHERS

SAROJINI NAIDU

Rise, brothers, rise; the waking skies pray to the morning
    light,
The wind lies asleep in the arms of the dawn like a child that
    has cried all night;
Come, let us gather our nets from the shore and set our
    catamarans free

[131]

To capture the leaping wealth of the tide, for we are the kings
of the sea!

No longer delay, let us hasten away in the track of the sea-
gull's call,
The sea is our mother, the cloud is our brother, the waves are
our comrades all,
What though we toss at the fall of the sun where the hand of
the sea-god drives?
He who holds the storm by the hair will hide in his breast our
lives.

Sweet is the shade of the cocoanut glade and the scent of the
mango grove,
And sweet are the sands at the fall of the moon with the
sound of the voices we love;
But sweeter, O brothers, the kiss of the spray, and the dance
of the wild foam's glee;
Row, brothers, row, to the blue of the verge, where the low
sky mates with the sea.

*The Coromandel Coast of India—the west shore of the Bay of Ben-
gal—is very treacherous. The native fishermen ply the waters fearlessly
in their catamarans, which are swift craft, consisting of three logs lashed
together and a crude sail.*

A SEA SONG

ALLAN CUNNINGHAM

A wet sheet and a flowing sea,
   A wind that follows fast,
And fills the white and rustling sail
   And bends the gallant mast;
And bends the gallant mast, my boys,

While, like the eagle free,
Away the good ship flies, and leaves
Old England on the lee.

O for a soft and gentle wind!
I heard a fair one cry;
But give to me the snoring breeze
And white waves heaving high;
And white waves heaving high, my lads,
The good ship tight and free—
The world of waters is our home,
And merry men are we.

There's tempest in yon hornèd moon,
And lightning in yon cloud;
But hark the music, mariners!
The wind is piping loud;
The wind is piping loud, my boys,
The lightning flashes free—
While the hollow oak our palace is,
Our heritage the sea.

*Allan Cunningham was a Scotch boy who was apprenticed to a stone
mason. He did not care for this work, but loved to make verses and
wanted to go to London and become a writer. This he accomplished,
though not till he was thirty years old.*

THE SEA GYPSY

RICHARD HOVEY

I am fevered with the sunset,
I am fretful with the bay,
For the wander-thirst is on me
And my soul is in Cathay.

The Sea Gypsy

There's a schooner in the offing,
With her top-sails shot with fire,
And my heart has gone aboard her
For the Islands of Desire.

I must forth again tomorrow!
With the sunset I must be,
Hull down on the trail of rapture
In the wonder of the Sea.

BEECH TREES

SISTER MARY MADELEVA

I passed a wood of beech trees yesterday
And I am shaken with its beauty yet.
Why should my breath catch and my eyes be wet
Because a hundred trees some yards away
Know simply how to dress in simple gray,
Are poised beyond the need of epithet
And beautiful past power to forget?
I dare not think how they will look in May.

They wore illustrious yellow in the fall.
Their beauty is no thing at which they guess.
And when they put on green, and when they carry
Fans open in sun or folded small,
I'll look through tears at ultimate loveliness:
Beeches in May, beeches in February.

The beech wood that inspired these lines is not far from the Holy Cross Convent in Indianapolis.

GOING DOWN HILL ON A BICYCLE

HENRY CHARLES BEECHING

With lifted feet, hands still,
I am poised, and down the hill
Dart, with heedful mind;
The air goes by in a wind.

Swifter and yet more swift,
Till the heart with a mighty lift
Makes the lungs laugh, the throat cry:—
"O bird, see; see, bird, I fly.

"Is this, is this your joy?
O bird, then I, though a boy,
For a golden moment share
Your feathery life in air!"

Say, heart, is there aught like this
In a world that is full of bliss?
'Tis more than skating, bound
Steel-shod to the level ground.

Speed slackens now, I float
Awhile in my airy boat;
Till, when the wheels scarce crawl,
My feet to the treadles fall.

Alas, that the longest hill
Must end in a vale; but still,
Who climbs with toil, whensoe'er,
Shall find wings waiting there.

PRAYER FOR A PILOT

CECIL ROBERTS

Lord of Sea and Earth and Air,
Listen to the Pilot's prayer—
Send him wind that's steady and strong,
Grant that his engine sings the song
Of flawless tone, by which he knows
It shall not fail him where he goes;
Landing, gliding, in curve, half-roll—
Grant him, O Lord, a full control,
That he may learn in heights of Heaven
The rapture altitude has given,
That he shall know the joy they feel
Who ride Thy realms on Birds of Steel.

Cecil Roberts is an Englishman who was an official war correspondent with the Royal Air Force during the First World War.

VISIONS

EDMUND LEAMY

I never watch the sun set a-down the Western skies
But that within its wonderness I see my mother's eyes;
I never hear the West wind sob softly in the trees
But that there comes her broken call far o'er the distant seas,
And never shine the dim stars but that my heart would go
Away and back to olden lands and dreams of long ago.

A rover of the wide world, when yet my heart was young,
The sea came whispering to me in well-beloved tongue,
And oh, the promises she held of golden lands a-gleam

That clung about my boy heart and filled mine eyes with
    dream,
And Wanderlust came luring me till 'neath the stars I swore
That I would be a wanderer for ever, ever more.

A rover of the wide world, I've seen the Northern lights
A-flashing countless colors in the knife-cold wintry nights;
I've watched the Southern Cross a-blaze o'er smiling, sunny
    lands,
And seen the lazy sea caress palm-sheltered, silver sands;
Still wild unrest is scourging me, the Wanderlust of yore,
And I must be a wanderer for ever, ever more.

And yet, I see the sun set a-down the Western skies,
And glimpse within the wonderness my mother's pleading
    eyes;
And yet, I hear the West wind sob softly in the trees
That vainly cloak her broken call far o'er the distant seas;
And still when shine the dim stars my wander-heart would go
Away and back to her side, and dreams of long ago.

OLD SHIPS

DAVID MORTON

There is a memory stays upon old ships,
    A weightless cargo in the musty hold,—
Of bright lagoons and prow-caressing lips,
    Of stormy midnights,—and a tale untold.
They have remembered islands in the dawn,
    And windy capes that tried their slender spars,
And tortuous channels where their keels have gone,
    And calm blue nights of stillness and the stars.

Old Ships

Ah, never think that ships forget a shore,
　Or bitter seas, or winds that made them wise;
There is a dream upon them, evermore;—
　And there be some who say that sunk ships rise
To seek familiar harbors in the night,
　Blowing in mists, their spectral sails like light.

HOME THOUGHTS FROM ABROAD

ROBERT BROWNING

Browning was a great traveler. He wrote this poem in Italy, the country he loved best, next to England.

Oh, to be in England
Now that April's there,
And whoever wakes in England
Sees, some morning, unaware,
That the lowest boughs and the brush-wood sheaf
Round the elm-tree bole are in tiny leaf,
While the chaffinch sings on the orchard bough
In England—now!

And after April, when May follows,
And the whitethroat builds, and all the swallows!
Hark, where my blossomed pear-tree in the hedge
Leans to the field and scatters on the clover
Blossoms and dewdrops—at the bent spray's edge—
That's the wise thrush; he sings each song twice over,
Lest you should think he never could recapture
The first fine careless rapture!
And though the fields look rough with hoary dew,
All will be gay when noontide wakes anew
The buttercups, the little children's dower
Far brighter than this gaudy melon-flower!

A SONG OF SHERWOOD

ALFRED NOYES

Sherwood in the twilight, is Robin Hood awake?
Grey and ghostly shadows are gliding through the brake;
Shadows of the dappled deer, dreaming of the morn,
Dreaming of a shadowy man that winds a shadowy horn.

Robin Hood is here again; all his merry thieves
Hear a ghostly bugle-note shivering through the leaves,
Calling as he used to call, faint and far away,
In Sherwood, in Sherwood, about the break of day.

Merry, merry England has kissed the lips of June:
All the wings of fairyland were here beneath the moon;
Like a flight of rose-leaves fluttering in a mist
Of opal and ruby and pearl and amethyst.

Merry, merry England is waking as of old,
With eyes of blither hazel and hair of brighter gold;
For Robin Hood is here again beneath the bursting spray
In Sherwood, in Sherwood, about the break of day.

Love is in the greenwood building him a house
Of wild rose and hawthorn and honeysuckle boughs;
Love is in the greenwood: dawn is in the skies;
And Marian is waiting with a glory in her eyes.

Hark! the dazzled laverock climbs the golden steep:
Marian is waiting: is Robin Hood asleep?
Round the fairy grass-rings frolic elf and fay,
In Sherwood, in Sherwood, about the break of day.

A Song of Sherwood

Oberon, Oberon, rake away the gold,
Rake away the red leaves, roll away the mould,
Rake away the gold leaves, roll away the red,
And wake Will Scarlett from his leafy forest bed.

Friar Tuck and Little John are riding down together
With quarter staff and drinking can and grey goose-feather;
The dead are coming back again; the years are rolled away
In Sherwood, in Sherwood, about the break of day.

Softly over Sherwood the soft wind blows;
All the heart of England hid in every rose
Hears across the greenwood the sunny whisper leap,
Sherwood in the red dawn, is Robin Hood asleep?

Hark, the voice of England wakes him as of old
And, shattering the silence with a cry of brighter gold,
Bugles in the greenwood echo from the steep,
Sherwood in the red dawn, is Robin Hood asleep?

Where the deer are gliding down the shadowy glen,
All across the glades of fern he calls his merry men;
Doublets of the Lincoln green glancing through the May
In Sherwood, in Sherwood, about the break of day.

Calls them and they answer: from aisles of oak and ash
Rings the *Follow! Follow!* and boughs begin to crash;
The ferns begin to flutter and the flowers begin to fly;
And through the crimson dawning the robber band goes by.

Robin! Robin! Robin! All his merry thieves
Answer as the bugle-note shivers through the leaves:
Calling as he used to call, faint and far away,
In Sherwood, in Sherwood, about the break of day.

JUNE

JAMES RUSSELL LOWELL

*This is an extract from Lowell's story poem, "The Vision of Sir
Launfal," which tells of an adventure of one of King Arthur's knights.*

And what is so rare as a day in June?
  Then, if ever, come perfect days;
Then Heaven tries the earth if it be in tune,
  And over it softly her warm ear lays;
Whether we look, or whether we listen,
We hear life murmur, or see it glisten;
Every clod feels a stir of might,
  An instinct within it that reaches and towers,
And, groping blindly above it for light,
  Climbs to a soul in grass and flowers;
The flush of life may well be seen
  Thrilling back over hills and valleys;
The cowslip startles in meadows green,
  The buttercup catches the sun in its chalice,
And there's never a leaf nor a blade too mean
  To be some happy creature's palace;
The little bird sits at his door in the sun,
  Atilt like a blossom among the leaves,
And lets his illumined being o'errun
  With the deluge of summer it receives;
His mate feels the eggs beneath her wings,
And the heart in her dumb breast flutters and sings;
He sings to the wide world and she to her nest—
In the nice ear of Nature, which song is the best?

Now is the high-tide of the year,
  And whatever of life hath ebbed away
Comes flooding back with a ripply cheer,

Into every bare inlet and creek and bay;
Now the heart is so full that a drop overfills it,
We are happy now because God wills it;
No matter how barren the past may have been,
'Tis enough for us now that the leaves are green;
We sit in the warm shade and feel right well
How the sap creeps up and the blossoms swell;
We may shut our eyes, but we cannot help knowing
That skies are clear and grass is growing;
The breeze comes whispering in our ear,
That dandelions are blossoming near,
That maize has sprouted, that streams are flowing,
That the river is bluer than the sky,
That the robin is plastering his house hard by;
And if the breeze kept the good news back,
For other couriers we should not lack;
We could guess it all by yon heifer's lowing,—
And hark! how clear bold chanticleer,
Warmed with the new wine of the year,
Tells all in his lusty crowing!

HIAWATHA'S SAILING

HENRY WADSWORTH LONGFELLOW

Give me of your bark, O Birch-Tree!
Of your yellow bark, O Birch-Tree!
Growing by the rushing river,
Tall and stately in the valley!
I a light canoe will build me,
Build a swift Cheemaun for sailing,
That shall float upon the river,
Like a yellow leaf in Autumn,
Like a yellow water-lily!

Lay aside your cloak, O Birch-tree!
Lay aside your white-skin wrapper,
For the summer-time is coming,
And the sun is warm in heaven,
And you need no white-skin wrapper!"

    Thus aloud cried Hiawatha
In the solitary forest,
By the rushing Taquamenaw,
When the birds were singing gayly,
In the Moon of Leaves were singing,
And the sun, from sleep awaking,
Started up and said, "Behold me!
Geezis, the great Sun, behold me!"
    And the tree with all its branches
Rustled in the breeze of morning,
Saying, with a sigh of patience,
"Take my cloak, O Hiawatha!"
    With his knife the tree he girdled;
Just beneath its lowest branches,
Just above the roots he cut it,
Till the sap came oozing outward;
Down the trunk from top to bottom,
Sheer he cleft the bark asunder,
With a wooden wedge he raised it,
Stripped it from the trunk unbroken.

    "Give me of your boughs, O Cedar!
Of your strong and pliant branches,
My canoe to make more steady,
Make more strong and firm beneath me!"
    Through the summit of the Cedar
Went a sound, a cry of horror,
Went a murmur of resistance;
But it whispered, bending downward,

"Take my boughs, O Hiawatha!"
Down he hewed the boughs of cedar,
Shaped them straightway to a framework,
Like two bows he formed and shaped them,
Like two bended bows together.

"Give me of your roots, O Tamarack!
Of your fibrous roots, O Larch-Tree!
My canoe to bind together,
So to bind the ends together
That the water may not enter,
That the river may not wet me!"
And the Larch, with all its fibers,
Shivered in the air of morning,
Touched his forehead with its tassels,
Said, with one long sigh of sorrow,
"Take them all, O Hiawatha!"
From the earth he tore the fibers,
Tore the tough roots of the Larch-Tree,
Closely sewed the bark together,
Bound it closely to the framework.

"Give me of your balm, O Fir-Tree!
Of your balsam and your resin,
So to close the seams together
That the water may not enter,
That the river may not wet me!"
And the fir-tree, tall and sombre,
Sobbed through all its robes of darkness,
Rattled like a shore with pebbles,
Answered wailing, answered weeping,
"Take my balm, O Hiawatha!"
And he took the tears of balsam,
Took the resin of the Fir-Tree,
Smeared therewith each seam and fissure,
Made each crevice safe from water.

"Give me of your quills, O Hedgehog!
All your quills, O Kagh, the Hedgehog!
I will make a necklace of them,
Make a girdle for my beauty,
And two stars to deck her bosom!"
From a hollow tree the Hedgehog
With his sleepy eyes looked at him,
Shot his shining quills like arrows,
Saying, with a drowsy murmur,
Through the tangle of his whiskers,
"Take my quills, O Hiawatha!"
From the ground the quills he gathered,
All the little shining arrows,
Stained them red and blue and yellow,
With the juice of roots and berries;
Into his canoe he wrought them,
Round its waist a shining girdle,
Round its bows a gleaming necklace,
On its breast two stars resplendent.

Thus the birch canoe was builded
In the valley, by the river,
In the bosom of the forest;
And the forest's life was in it,
All its mystery and its magic,
All the lightness of the Birch-Tree,
All the toughness of the Cedar,
All the Larch's supple sinews;
And it floated on the river
Like a yellow leaf in Autumn,
Like a yellow water-lily.

Paddles none had Hiawatha,
Paddles none he had or needed,
For his thoughts as paddles served him,
And his wishes served to guide him;

Swift or slow at will he glided,
Veered to right or left at pleasure.
    Then he called aloud to Kwasind,
To his friend, the strong man, Kwasind,
Saying, "Help me clear this river
Of its sunken logs and sand-bars."
    Straight into the river Kwasind
Plunged as if he were an otter,
Dived as if he were a beaver,
Stood up to his waist in water,
To his arm-pits in the river,
Swam and shouted in the river,
Tugged at sunken logs and branches,
With his hands he scooped the sand-bars,
With his feet the ooze and tangle.
    And thus sailed my Hiawatha
Down the rushing Taquamenaw,
Sailed through all its bends and windings,
Sailed through all its deeps and shallows,
While his friend, the strong man, Kwasind,
Swam the deeps, the shallows waded.
    Up and down the river went they,
In and out among its islands,
Cleared its bed of root and sand-bar,
Dragged the dead trees from its channel,
Made its passage safe and certain,
Made a pathway for the people,
From its springs among the mountains,
To the waters of Pauwating,
To the bay of Taquamenaw.

THE MODERN HIAWATHA

ANONYMOUS

When he killed the Mudjokivis,
Of the skin he made him mittens,
Made them with the fur side inside,
Made them with the skin side outside,
He, to get the warm side inside,
Put the inside skin side outside;
He, to get the cold side outside,
Put the warm side fur side inside.
That's why he put fur side inside,
Why he put the skin side outside,
Why he turned the inside outside.

NOVEMBER

THOMAS HOOD

No sun—no moon!
No morn—no noon—
No dawn—no dusk—no proper time of day—
No sky—no earthly view—
No distance looking blue—
No road—no street—no "t'other side the way"—
No end to any Row—
No indications where the crescents go—
No top to any steeple—
No recognitions of familiar people—
No courtesies for showing 'em—
No knowing 'em!
No traveling at all—no locomotion—
No inkling of the way—no notion
"No go"—by land or ocean—

No mail—no post—
No news from any foreign coast—
No park—no ring—no afternoon gentility—
No company—no nobility—
No warmth, no cheerfulness, no healthful ease,
No comfortable feel in any member—
No shade, no shine, no butterflies, no bees,
No fruits, no flowers, no leaves, no birds—
November!

SNOW-FLAKES

HENRY WADSWORTH LONGFELLOW

Out of the bosom of the Air,
 Out of the cloud-folds of her garments shaken,
Over the woodlands brown and bare,
 Over the harvest-fields forsaken,
  Silent and soft and slow
  Descends the snow.

Even as our cloudy fancies take
 Suddenly shape in some divine expression,
Even as the troubled heart doth make
 In the white countenance confession,
  The troubled sky reveals
  The grief it feels.

This is the poem of the air,
 Slowly in silent syllables recorded;
This is the secret of despair,
 Long in its cloudy bosom hoarded,
  Now whispered and revealed
  To wood and field.

Part Three

POEMS OF PEACE AND WAR

※ᵔᵕᵔ ᵕᵔ※

Keep heart, O comrade, God may be delayed
By Evil, but He suffers no defeat.
God is not foiled. The drift of the World will
Is stronger than all wrong.

Walt Whitman

I HAVE A RENDEZVOUS WITH DEATH

ALAN SEEGER

I have a rendezvous with Death
    At some disputed barricade
    When Spring comes round with rustling shade
And apple blossoms fill the air.
    I have a rendezvous with Death
When Spring brings back blue days and fair.

It may be he shall take my hand
And lead me into his dark land
    And close my eyes and quench my breath;
It may be I shall pass him, still,
    I have a rendezvous with Death
On some scarred slope of battered hill,
    When Spring comes round again this year
    And the first meadow flowers appear.

God knows 'twere better to be deep
    Pillowed in silk and scented down,
Where love throbs out in blissful sleep,
    Pulse nigh to pulse, and breath to breath,
Where hushed awakenings are dear . . .
    But I've a rendezvous with Death
        At midnight in some flaming town,
When Spring trips north again this year,
    And I to my pledged word am true,
    I shall not fail that rendezvous.

Alan Seeger was a New York boy who, in 1914, joined the Foreign Legion, "that most famous, most reckless, most courageous regiment in the world," and fell in France while charging the German trenches at Belloy-en-Santerre. They took the village but next morning Alan Seeger lay dead, having kept his rendezvous. He was twenty-eight years old.

IN FLANDERS FIELDS

JOHN McCRAE

This poem, written in the spring of 1915, after the terrible battles of Ypres, expresses very truly how men felt in those days of the First World War. It was first published in "Punch" and at once became popular in the armies and the war-torn world. John McCrae was a young Canadian doctor who lost his life in service in Flanders in January, 1918.

In Flanders fields the poppies blow
   Between the crosses, row on row,
That mark our place; and in the sky
   The larks, still bravely singing, fly
Scarce heard amid the guns below.

We are the dead. Short days ago
   We lived, felt dawn, saw sunset glow,
Loved and were loved, and now we lie
   In Flanders fields.

Take up our quarrel with the foe;
   To you from failing hands we throw
The torch; be yours to hold it high,
   If ye break faith with us who die
We shall not sleep, though poppies grow
   In Flanders fields.

THE SOLDIER

RUPERT BROOKE

If I should die, think only this of me:
   That there's some corner of a foreign field
That is for ever England. There shall be
   In that rich earth a richer earth concealed;
A dust whom England bore, shaped, made aware,
   Gave, once, her flowers to love, her ways to roam,

A body of England's, breathing English air,
  Washed by the rivers, blest by suns of home.

And think, this heart, all evil shed away,
  A pulse in the eternal mind, no less
Gives somewhere back the thoughts by England given;
  Her sights and sounds; dreams happy as her day;
And laughter learnt of friends; and gentleness,
  In hearts at peace under an English heaven.

There is a spot in an olive grove on the island of Scyros, in the Ægean Sea, that is "forever England." There Rupert Brooke lies buried. He went to war in September, 1914, with the Royal Navy, and died on April 23, 1915, at the age of twenty-seven.

HIGH FLIGHT

JOHN GILLESPIE MAGEE, JR.

Oh, I have slipped the surly bonds of earth,
And danced the skies on laughter-silvered wings;
Sunward I've climbed and joined the tumbling mirth
Of sun-split clouds—and done a hundred things
You have not dreamed of—wheeled and soared and swung
High in the sunlit silence. Hov'ring there,
I've chased the shouting wind along and flung
My eager craft through footless halls of air.
Up, up the long delirious, burning blue
I've topped the wind-swept heights with easy grace,
Where never lark, or even eagle, flew;
And, while with silent, lifting mind I've trod
The high untrespassed sanctity of space,
Put out my hand, and touched the face of God.

This poem was written by a nineteen-year-old citizen of the United States just before he was killed in action with the Royal Canadian Air Force, December, 1941. Poets hailed it as the first classic of the Second World War.

ULTIMA RATIO REGUM

STEPHEN SPENDER

The guns spell money's ultimate reason
In letters of lead on the spring hillside.
But the boy lying dead under the olive trees
Was too young and too silly
To have been notable to their important eye.
He was a better target for a kiss.

When he lived, tall factory hooters never summoned him.
Nor did restaurant plate-glass doors revolve to wave him in.
His name never appeared in the papers.
The world maintained its traditional wall
Round the dead with their gold sunk deep as a well,
Whilst his life, intangible as a Stock Exchange rumour,
    drifted outside.

O too lightly he threw down his cap
One day when the breeze threw petals from the trees.
The unflowering wall sprouted with guns,
Machine-gun anger quickly scythed the grasses;
Flags and leaves fell from hands and branches;
The tweed cap rotted in the nettles.

Consider his life which was valueless
In terms of employment, hotel ledgers, news files.
Consider. One bullet in ten thousand kills a man.
Ask. Was so much expenditure justified
On the death of one so young and so silly
Lying under the olive trees, O world, O death?

*Stephen Spender is an English poet and critic, born in 1909. He
has lived and taught in the United States.*

HORATIUS AT THE BRIDGE

THOMAS BABINGTON MACAULAY

Macaulay, an Englishman living in 1842, wrote this poem as though it were told by a Roman in about 390 B. C., dealing with an event in Roman history of about 510 B. C. It is one of his "Lays of Ancient Rome."

Lars Porsena of Clusium,
   By the Nine Gods he swore
That the great house of Tarquin
   Should suffer wrong no more.
By the Nine Gods he swore it,
   And named a trysting day.
And bade his messengers ride forth,
East and west and south and north,
   To summon his array.

East and west and south and north
   The messengers ride fast,
And tower and town and cottage
   Have heard the trumpet's blast.
Shame on the false Etruscan
   Who lingers in his home,
When Porsena of Clusium
   Is on the march for Rome!

The horsemen and the footmen
   Are pouring in amain,
From many a stately market-place,
   From many a fruitful plain;

.   .   .   .

And now hath every city
   Sent up her tale of men;
The foot are fourscore thousand,

[155]

The horse are thousands ten;
Before the gates of Sutrium
  Is met the great array;
A proud man was Lars Porsena
  Upon the trysting-day.

.   .   .   .

But by the yellow Tiber
  Was tumult and affright;
From all the spacious champaign
  To Rome men took their flight.
A mile around the city
  The throng stopped up the ways;
A fearful sight it was to see
  Through two long nights and days:

.   .   .   .

Now, from the rock Tarpeian,
  Could the wan burghers spy
The line of blazing villages
  Red in the midnight sky.
The Fathers of the City,
  They sat all night and day,
For every hour some horseman came
  With tidings of dismay.

.   .   .   .

They held a council standing
  Before the River Gate;
Short time was there, ye well may guess,
  For musing or debate.
Out spoke the Consul roundly:
  "The bridge must straight go down;
For, since Janiculum is lost,
  Naught else can save the town."

Just then a scout came flying,
  All wild with haste and fear:

"To arms! to arms! Sir Consul;
  Lars Porsena is here."
On the low hills to westward
  The Consul fixed his eye,
And saw the swarthy storm of dust
  Rise fast along the sky.

And nearer, fast, and nearer
  Doth the red whirlwind come;
And louder still, and still more loud,
From underneath that rolling cloud,
Is heard the trumpet's war-note proud,
  The trampling and the hum.
And plainly and more plainly
  Now through the gloom appears,
Far to left and far to right,
In broken gleams of dark-blue light,
The long array of helmets bright,
  The long array of spears.

.   .   .   .

But the Consul's brow was sad,
  And the Consul's speech was low,
And darkly looked he at the wall,
  And darkly at the foe:
"Their van will be upon us
  Before the bridge goes down;
And if they once may win the bridge
  What hope to save the town?"

Then outspake brave Horatius,
  The captain of the gate:
"To every man upon this earth
  Death cometh soon or late.
And how can man die better
  Than facing fearful odds

For the ashes of his fathers
    And the temples of his gods?

"Hew down the bridge, Sir Consul,
    With all the speed ye may;
I, with two more to help me,
    Will hold the foe in play,—
In yon strait path a thousand
    May well be stopped by three.
Now who will stand on either hand,
    And keep the bridge with me?"

Then out spake Spurius Lartius,—
    A Ramnian proud was he:
"Lo, I will stand at thy right hand,
    And keep the bridge with thee."
And out spake strong Herminius,—
    Of Titian blood was he:
"I will abide on thy left side,
    And keep the bridge with thee."

"Horatius," quoth the Consul,
    "As thou sayest, so let it be."
And straight against that great array,
    Forth went the dauntless Three.

  .   .   .   .

Now, while the Three were tightening
    Their harness on their backs,
The Consul was the foremost man
    To take in hand an axe;
And Fathers mixed with Commons
    Seized hatchet, bar, and crow,
And smote upon the planks above,
    And loosed the props below.

Meanwhile the Tuscan army,
  Right glorious to behold,
Came flashing back the noonday light,
Rank behind rank, like surges bright
  Of a broad sea of gold.
Four hundred trumpets sounded
  A peal of warlike glee,
As that great host, with measured tread,
And spears advanced, and ensigns spread,
Rolled slowly toward the bridge's head,
  Where stood the dauntless Three.

The Three stood calm and silent,
  And looked upon the foes,
And a great shout of laughter
  From all the vanguard rose:
And forth three chiefs came spurring
  Before that deep array;
To earth they sprang, their swords they drew,
And lifted high their shields, and flew
  To win the narrow way;
Aunus from green Tifernum,
  Lord of the Hill of Vines;
And Seius, whose eight hundred slaves
  Sicken in Ilva's mines;
And Picus, long to Clusium
  Vassal in peace and war.

Stout Lartius hurled down Aunus
  Into the stream beneath;
Herminius struck at Seius,
  And clove him to the teeth;
At Picus brave Horatius
  Darted one fiery thrust;

And the proud Umbrian's golden arms
   Clashed in the bloody dust.

"Lie there," he cried, "fell pirate!
   No more, aghast and pale,
From Ostia's walls the crowd shall mark
The track of thy destroying bark;
No more Campania's hinds shall fly
To woods and caverns, when they spy
   Thy thrice-accursed sail!"

But now no sound of laughter
   Was heard among the foes;
A wild and wrathful clamor
   From all the vanguard rose.
Six spears' lengths from the entrance
   Halted that deep array,
And for a space no man came forth
   To win the narrow way.

But hark! the cry is Astur:
   And lo! the ranks divide;
And the great Lord of Luna
   Comes with his stately stride.
Upon his stately shoulders
   Clangs loud the fourfold shield,
And in his hand he shakes the brand
   Which none but he can wield.

He smiled on those bold Romans,
   A smile serene and high;
He eyed the flinching Tuscans,
   And scorn was in his eye.
Quoth he, "The she-wolf's litter
   Stand savagely at bay;

But will ye dare to follow,
   If Astur clears the way?"

Then, swirling up his broadsword
   With both hands to the height,
He rushed against Horatius,
   And smote with all his might,
With shield and blade Horatius
   Right deftly turned the blow,
The blow, though turned, came yet too nigh;
It missed his helm, but gashed his thigh,
The Tuscans raised a joyful cry
   To see the red blood flow.

He reeled, and on Herminius
   He leaned one breathing-space,
Then, like a wild-cat mad with wounds,
   Sprang right at Astur's face.
Through teeth and skull and helmet
   So fierce a thrust he sped,
The good sword stood a handbreadth out
   Behind the Tuscan's head.

And the great lord of Luna
   Fell at that deadly stroke,
As falls on Mount Avernus
   A thunder-smitten oak.
Far o'er the crashing forest
   The giant arms lie spread;
And the pale augurs, muttering low,
   Gaze on the blasted head.

On Astur's throat Horatius
   Right firmly pressed his heel,
And thrice and four times tugged amain,

[161]

Ere he wrenched out the steel.
"And see," he cried, "the welcome,
    Fair guests, that waits you here!
What noble Lucumo comes next
    To taste our Roman cheer?"

.   .   .   .

But meanwhile axe and lever
    Have manfully been plied,
And now the bridge hangs tottering
    Above the boiling tide.
"Come back, come back, Horatius!"
    Loud cried the Fathers all.
"Back, Lartius! Back, Herminius!
    Back, ere the ruin fall!"

Back darted Spurius Lartius;
    Herminius darted back:
And, as they passed, beneath their feet
    They felt the timbers crack.
But when they turned their faces,
    And on the farther shore
Saw brave Horatius stand alone,
    They would have crossed once more.

But with a crash like thunder
    Fell every loosened beam,
And, like a dam, the mighty wreck
    Lay right athwart the stream;
And a long shout of triumph
    Rose from the walls of Rome,
As to the highest turret tops
    Was splashed the yellow foam.

And, like a horse unbroken
    When first he feels the rein,

The furious river struggled hard,
　　And tossed his tawny mane.
And burst the curb and bounded,
　　Rejoicing to be free,
And whirling down, in fierce career,
Battlement, and plank, and pier,
　　Rushed headlong to the sea.

Alone stood brave Horatius,
　　But constant still in mind;
Thrice thirty thousand foes before,
　　And the broad flood behind.
"Down with him!" cried false Sextus,
　　With a smile on his pale face.
"Now yield thee," cried Lars Porsena,
　　"Now yield thee to our grace."

Round turned he, as not deigning
　　Those craven ranks to see;
Naught spake he to Lars Porsena,
　　To Sextus naught spake he;
But he saw on Palatinus
　　The white porch of his home;
And he spake to the noble river
　　That rolls by the towers of Rome:

"O Tiber! Father Tiber!
　　To whom the Romans pray,
A Roman's life, a Roman's arms,
　　Take thou in charge this day!"
So he spake, and, speaking, sheathed
　　The good sword by his side,
And, with his harness on his back,
　　Plunged headlong in the tide.

No sound of joy or sorrow
    Was heard from either bank,
But friends and foes in dumb surprise,
With parted lips and straining eyes,
    Stood gazing where he sank;
And when above the surges
    They saw his crest appear,
All Rome sent forth a rapturous cry,
And even the ranks of Tuscany
    Could scarce forbear to cheer.

But fiercely ran the current,
    Swollen high by months of rain,
And fast his blood was flowing;
    And he was sore in pain,
And heavy with his armor,
    And spent with changing blows;
And oft they thought him sinking,
    But still again he rose.

.   .   .   .

Never, I ween, did swimmer,
    In such an evil case,
Struggle through such a raging flood
    Safe to the landing place;
But his limbs were borne up bravely
    By the brave heart within,
And our good father Tiber
    Bare bravely up his chin.

"Curse on him," quoth false Sextus,
    "Will not the villain drown?
But for this stay, ere close of day
    We should have sacked the town!"
"Heaven help him," quoth Lars Porsena,
    "And bring him safe to shore;

For such a gallant feat of arms
    Was never seen before."

And now he feels the bottom;——
    Now on dry earth he stands;
Now round him throng the Fathers
    To press his gory hands.
And, now, with shouts and clapping,
    And noise of weeping loud,
He enters through the River Gate,
    Borne by the joyous crowd.

SAINT GEORGE OF ENGLAND

CECILY FOX-SMITH

Saint George he was a fighting man, as all the tales do tell;
He fought a battle long ago, and fought it wondrous well.
With his helmet, and his hauberk, and his good cross-hilted
    sword,
Oh, he rode a-slaying dragons to the glory of the Lord.
And when his time on earth was done, he found he could not
    rest
Where the year is always summer in the Islands of the Blest;
So back he came to earth again, to see what he could do,
And they cradled him in England—
        In England, April England—
Oh, they cradled him in England where the golden willows
    blew!

Saint George he was a fighting man, and loved a fighting
    breed,
And whenever England wants him now, he's ready at her
    need;

From Crecy field to Neuve Chapelle he's there with hand and
    sword,
And he sailed with Drake from Devon to the glory of the
    Lord.
His arm is strong to smite the wrong and break the tyrant's
    pride,
He was there when Nelson triumphed, he was there when
    Gordon died;
He sees his red-cross ensign float on all the winds that blow,
But ah! his heart's in England—
       In England, April England—
Oh, his heart it turns to England where the golden willows
    grow.

Saint George he was a fighting man, he's here and fighting
    still
While any wrong is yet to right or Dragon yet to kill.
And faith! he's finding work this day to suit his war-worn
    sword,
For he's strafing Huns in Flanders to the glory of the Lord.
Saint George he is a fighting man, but when the fighting's
    past,
And dead among the trampled fields the fiercest and the last
Of all the Dragons earth has known beneath his feet lies low,
Oh, his heart will turn to England—
       To England, April England—
He'll come home to rest in England where the golden willows
    blow!

KING HENRY BEFORE THE FIELD
OF SAINT CRISPIAN

WILLIAM SHAKESPEARE

The speech with which King Henry rallied his soldiers before a
battle in which they were outnumbered five to one by the enemy.

If we are marked to die, we are enow
To do our country loss; and if to live,
The fewer men, the greater share of honour.
God's will! I pray thee, wish not one man more.
By Jove, I am not covetous for gold,
Nor care I who doth feed upon my cost;
It yearns me not if men my garments wear;
Such outward things dwell not in my desires.
But if it be a sin to covet honour,
I am the most offending soul alive.
No, faith, my coz, wish not a man from England:
God's peace! I would not lose so great an honour
As one man more, methinks, would share from me
For the best hope I have. O, do not wish one more!
Rather proclaim it, Westmoreland, through my host,
That he which hath no stomach to this fight,
Let him depart; his passport shall be made
And crowns for convoy put into his purse:
We would not die in that man's company
That fears his fellowship to die with us.
This day is called the feast of Crispian;
He that outlives this day, and comes safe home,
Will stand atip-toe when this day is named,
And rouse him at the name of Crispian.
He that shall live this day, and see old age,
Will yearly on the vigil feast his neighbours,
And say, 'To-morrow is Saint Crispian:'

Then will he strip his sleeve and show his scars,
And say, 'These wounds I had on Crispin's day.'
Old men forget: yet all shall be forgot,
  But he'll remember with advantages
  What feats he did that day: then shall our names,
  Familiar in his mouth as household words,
  Harry the king, Bedford and Exeter,
  Warwick and Talbot, Salisbury and Gloucester,
  Be in their flowing cups freshly remembered.
  This story shall the good man teach his son;
  And Crispin Crispian shall ne'er go by,
  From this day to the ending of the world,
  But we in it shall be remembered;
    We few, we happy few, we band of brothers;
  For he to-day who sheds his blood with me
  Shall be my brother; be he ne'er so vile,
  This day shall gentle his condition:
  And gentlemen in England now a-bed
  Shall think themselves accursed they were not here,
  And hold their manhoods cheap whiles any speaks
  That fought with us upon Saint Crispian's day.

From *King Henry V*

AFTER BLENHEIM

ROBERT SOUTHEY

Blenheim, in Bavaria, was the scene of "the famous victory" of the Duke of Marlborough and Prince Eugene, over the French and Bavarians, on August 13, 1704. Of 56,000 French and Bavarians, 14,000 were taken prisoner and 25,000 perished by the sword or in the Danube. The victors lost 5,000 killed and 8,000 wounded.

It was a summer's evening,
    Old Kaspar's work was done,
And he before his cottage door
    Was sitting in the sun;
And by him sported on the green
His little grandchild, Wilhelmine.

She saw her brother Peterkin
    Roll something large and round,
Which he beside the rivulet,
    In playing there, had found.
He came to ask what he had found,
That was so large, and smooth, and round.

Old Kasper took it from the boy,
    Who stood expectant by;
And then the old man shook his head,
    And, with a natural sigh,
" 'Tis some poor fellow's skull," said he,
"Who fell in the great victory!

"I find them in the garden,
    For there's many hereabout;
And often, when I go to plow,
    The plowshare turns them out;
For many thousand men," said he,
"Were slain in that great victory!"

After Blenheim

"Now tell us what 'twas all about,"
    Young Peterkin he cries;
And little Wilhelmine looks up
    With wonder-waiting eyes;
"Now tell us all about the war,
And what they killed each other for?"

"It was the English," Kaspar cried,
    "Who put the French to rout;
But what they killed each other for
    I could not well make out.
But every body said," quoth he,
"That 'twas a famous victory!

"My father lived at Blenheim then,
    Yon little stream hard by;
They burned his dwelling to the ground,
    And he was forced to fly;
So with his wife and child he fled,
Nor had he where to rest his head.

"With fire and sword the country round
    Was wasted far and wide;
And many a childing mother then
    And new-born baby died.
But things like that, you know, must be,
At every famous victory.

"They say it was a shocking sight
    After the field was won;
For many thousand bodies here
    Lay rotting in the sun.
But things like that, you know, must be,
After a famous victory.

"Great praise the Duke of Marlborough won,
    And our good Prince Eugene."

"Why, 'twas a very wicked thing!"
    Said little Wilhelmine.
"Nay, nay, my little girl," quoth he,
"It was a famous victory!

"And every body praised the duke
    Who this great fight did win."
"But what good came of it at last?"
    Quoth little Peterkin.
"Why, that I cannot tell," said he,
"But 'twas a famous victory!"

THE *REVENGE*

ALFRED TENNYSON

It was in August, 1591, that the English fleet, lying in the Azores, en-counter ed fifty-three Spanish vessels of the famous Armada, sent out as escort to Spanish treasure galleons coming from the West Indies.

At Flores in the Azores Sir Richard Grenville lay,
And a pinnace, like a flutter'd bird, came flying from far
    away:
"Spanish ships of war at sea! we have sighted fifty-three!"
Then sware Lord Thomas Howard: "Fore God I am no
    coward;
But I can not meet them here, for my ships are out of gear,
And the half my men are sick. I must fly, but follow quick.
We are six ships of the line; can we fight with fifty-three?"
Then spake Sir Richard Grenville: "I know you are no
    coward;
You fly them for a moment to fight with them again.
But I've ninety men and more that are lying sick ashore.
I should count myself the coward if I left them, my Lord
    Howard,
To these Inquisition dogs and the devildoms of Spain."

The Revenge

So Lord Howard past away with five ships of war that day,
Till he melted like a cloud in the silent summer heaven;
But Sir Richard bore in hand all his sick men from the land
Very carefully and slow,
Men of Bideford in Devon,
And we laid them on the ballast down below;
For we brought them all aboard,
And they blest him in their pain, that they were not left to
    Spain,
To the thumbscrew and the stake, for the glory of the Lord.

He had only a hundred seamen to work the ship and to fight,
And he sailed away from Flores till the Spaniard came in
    sight,
With his huge sea-castles heaving upon the weather bow.
"Shall we fight or shall we fly?
Good Sir Richard, tell us now,
For to fight is but to die!
There'll be little of us left by the time this sun be set."
And Sir Richard said again: "We be all good English men.
Let us bang these dogs of Seville, the children of the devil,
For I never turn'd my back upon Don or devil yet."

Sir Richard spoke and he laugh'd, and we roar'd a hurrah,
    and so
The little *Revenge* ran on sheer into the heart of the foe,
With her hundred fighters on deck, and her ninety sick be-
    low;
For half of their fleet to the right and half to the left were
    seen,
And the little *Revenge* ran on thro' the long sea lane between.

Thousands of their soldiers look'd down from their decks
    and laugh'd,
Thousands of their seamen made mock at the mad little craft

Running on and on, till delay'd
By their mountain-like *San Philip* that, of fifteen hundred
    tons,
And up-shadowing high above us with her yawning tiers of
    guns,
Took the breath from our sails, and we stay'd.

And while now the great *San Philip* hung above us like a
    cloud
Whence the thunderbolt will fall
Long and loud,
Four galleons drew away
From the Spanish fleet that day,
And two upon the larboard and two upon the starboard lay,
And the battle-thunder broke from them all.

But anon the great *San Philip,* she bethought herself and
    went,
Having that within her womb that had left her ill content;
And the rest they came aboard us, and they fought us hand
    to hand,
For a dozen times they came with their pikes and musque-
    teers,
And a dozen times we shook 'em off as a dog that shakes his
    ears
When he leaps from the water to the land.

And the sun went down, and the stars came out far over the
    summer sea,
But never a moment ceased the fight of the one and the fifty-
    three;
Ship after ship, the whole night long, their high-built gal-
    leons came,
Ship after ship, the whole night long, with her battle-thunder
    and flame;

Ship after ship, the whole night long, drew back with her
  dead and her shame.
For some were sunk and many were shatter'd, and so could
  fight us no more—
God of battles, was ever a battle like this in the world before?
For he said "Fight on! fight on!"
Tho' his vessel was all but a wreck;
And it chanced that, when half of the short summer night
  was gone,
With a grisly wound to be drest he had left the deck,
But a bullet struck him that was dressing it suddenly dead,
And himself he was wounded again in the side and the head,
And he said "Fight on! fight on!"

And the night went down, and the sun smiled out far over
  the summer sea,
And the Spanish fleet with broken sides lay round us all in a
  ring;
But they dared not touch us again, for they fear'd that we
  still could sting,
So they watch'd what the end would be.
And we had not fought them in vain,
But in perilous plight were we,
Seeing forty of our poor hundred were slain,
And half of the rest of us maim'd for life
In the crash of the cannonades and the desperate strife;
And the sick men down in the hold were most of them stark
  and cold,
And the pikes were all broken or bent, and the powder was
  all of it spent;
And the masts and the rigging were lying over the side;
But Sir Richard cried in his English pride,
"We have fought such a fight for a day and a night

As may never be fought again!
We have won great glory, my men!
And a day less or more
At sea or ashore,
We die—does it matter when?
Sink me the ship, Master Gunner—sink her, split her in
    twain!
Fall into the hands of God, not into the hands of Spain!"
And the gunner said, "Ay, ay," but the seamen made reply:
"We have children, we have wives,
And the Lord hath spared our lives.
We will make the Spanish promise, if we yield, to let us go;
We shall live to fight again, and to strike another blow."
And the lion there lay dying, and they yielded to the foe.
And the stately Spanish men to their flagship bore him then,
Where they laid him by the mast, old Sir Richard caught at
    last,
And they praised him to his face with their courtly foreign
    grace;
But he rose upon their decks, and he cried:
"I have fought for Queen and Faith like a valiant man and
    true;
I have only done my duty as a man is bound to do.
With a joyful spirit I Sir Richard Grenville die!"
And he fell upon their decks, and he died.

And they stared at the dead that had been so valiant and true,
And had holden the power and the glory of Spain so cheap
That he dared her with one little ship and his English few;
Was he devil or man? He was devil for aught they knew,
But they sank his body with honor down into the deep,
And they mann'd the *Revenge* with a swarthier alien crew,
And away she sail'd with her loss and long'd for her own;

The Revenge

When a wind from the lands they had ruin'd awoke from
   sleep,
And the water began to heave and the weather to moan,
And or ever that evening ended a great gale blew,
And a wave like the wave that is raised by an earthquake
   grew,
Till it smote on their hulls and their sails and their masts and
   their flags,
And the whole sea plunged and fell on the shot-shatter'd navy
   of Spain,
And the little *Revenge* herself went down by the island crags
To be lost evermore in the main.

HAWKE

HENRY NEWBOLT

*Hawke was a famous English admiral of the eighteenth century. He
entered the Navy at fifteen. In November, 1759, he met the French pre-
paring to invade England, and fought a naval battle off Belle-Isle. Half
the French vessels, but only two of Hawke's were disabled.*

In seventeen hundred and fifty-nine,
   When Hawke came swooping from the West
The French King's Admiral with twenty of the line,
   Was sailing forth, to sack us, out of Brest.
The ports of France were crowded, the quays of France
   a-hum
   With thirty thousand soldiers marching to the drum,
For bragging time was over and fighting time was come
   When Hawke came swooping from the West.

'Twas long past noon of a wild November day
   When Hawke came swooping from the West;
He heard the breakers thundering in Quiberon Bay

[176]

But he flew the flag for battle, line abreast.
Down upon the quicksands, roaring out of sight
  Fiercely beat the storm-wind, darkly fell the night,
But they took the foe for pilot and the cannon's glare for
    light
  When Hawke came swooping from the West.

The Frenchmen turned like a covey down the wind
  When Hawke came swooping from the West;
One he sank with all hands, one he caught and pinned,
  And the shallows and the storm took the rest.
The guns that should have conquered us, they rusted on the
    shore,
  And the men that would have mastered us they drummed
    and marched no more,
For England was England and a mighty brood she bore
  When Hawke came swooping from the West.

THE BURIAL OF SIR JOHN MOORE

CHARLES WOLFE

*Sir John Moore was one of those rare immense characters and born
leaders who in his day in the early nineteenth century, was revered by
the entire British Army. His men held a deep affection for him.*

*The brave Sir John Moore fought a desperate battle with Napoleon
at Coruña in Spain on January 16, 1809. He had 25,000 men and Na-
poleon had 70,000. At an early stage of the battle Moore was struck by
a cannon ball and died in the moment of victory.*

Not a drum was heard, not a funeral note,
  As his corse to the rampart we hurried;
Not a soldier discharged his farewell shot
  O'er the grave where our hero we buried.

The Burial of Sir John Moore

We buried him darkly at dead of night,
   The sods with our bayonets turning;
By the struggling moonbeam's misty light,
   And the lantern dimly burning.

No useless coffin enclosed his breast,
   Not in sheet nor shroud we wound him;
But he lay like a warrior taking his rest,
   With his martial cloak around him.

Few and short were the prayers we said,
   And we spoke not a word of sorrow;
But we steadfastly gazed on the face that was dead,
   And we bitterly thought of the morrow.

We thought, as we hollow'd his narrow bed,
   And smoothed down his lonely pillow,
That the foe and the stranger would tread o'er his head,
   And we far away on the billow!

Lightly they'll talk of the spirit that's gone,
   And o'er his cold ashes upbraid him,—
But little he'll reck, if they let him sleep on
   In the grave where a Briton has laid him.

But half of our heavy task was done
   When the clock struck the hour for retiring;
And we heard the distant and random gun
   That the foe was sullenly firing.

Slowly and sadly we laid him down,
   From the field of his fame fresh and gory;
We carved not a line, and we raised not a stone—
   But we left him alone with his glory!

AN INCIDENT OF THE FRENCH CAMP

ROBERT BROWNING

You know we French stormed Ratisbon:
   A mile or so away,
On a little mound, Napoleon
   Stood on our storming day;
With neck out-thrust, you fancy how,
   Legs wide, arms locked behind,
As if to balance the prone brow
   Oppressive with its mind.

Just as perhaps he mused, "My plans
   That soar, to earth may fall
Let once my army-leader Lannes
   Waver at yonder wall,"—
Out 'twixt the battery-smokes there flew
   A rider, bound on bound
Full-galloping; nor bridle drew
   Until he reached the mound.

Then off there flung in smiling joy,
   And held himself erect
By just his horse's mane, a boy:
   You hardly could suspect—
(So tight he kept his lips compressed,
   Scarce any blood came through,)
You looked twice e'er you saw his breast,
   Was all but shot in two.

"Well," cried he, "Emperor, by God's grace
   We've got you Ratisbon!
The marshal's in the market-place,
   And you'll be there anon

[179]

To see your flag-bird flap his vans
  Where I, to heart's desire,
Perched him." The chief's eye flashed; his plans
  Soared up again like fire.

The chief's eye flashed; but presently
  Softened itself, as sheathes
A film the mother eagle's eye
  When her bruised eaglet breathes:
"You're wounded!" "Nay," his soldier's pride
  Touched to the quick, he said:
"I'm killed, sire!" And, his chief beside,
  Smiling, the boy fell dead.

THE EVE OF WATERLOO

GEORGE GORDON BYRON

June 18, 1815, is the famous day when Napoleon Bonaparte "met his Waterloo." This part of Byron's long poem, "Childe Harold," describes the scene at a ball in Brussels on the night of the seventeenth, when many of Wellington's officers were enjoying themselves, little dreaming of Napoleon's sudden attack. The battle, which took place in the morning and raged all day, resulted in the complete overthrow of Napoleon's power.

There was a sound of revelry by night,
And Belgium's capital had gathered then
Her Beauty and her Chivalry, and bright
The lamps shone o'er fair women and brave men;
A thousand hearts beat happily; and when
Music arose with its voluptuous swell,
Soft eyes looked love to eyes which spake again,
And all went merry as a marriage-bell;
But hush! hark! a deep sound strikes like a rising knell!

Did ye not hear it?—No; 'twas but the wind,
Or the car rattling o'er the stony street;
On with the dance! let joy be unconfined,
No sleep till morn, when Youth and Pleasure meet,
To chase the glowing Hours with flying feet—
But hark!—that heavy sound breaks in once more,
As if the clouds in echo would repeat;
And nearer, clearer, deadlier than before!
Arm! arm! it is—it is—the cannon's opening roar!

Ah! then and there was hurrying to and fro,
And gathering tears, and tremblings of distress,
And cheeks all pale, which but an hour ago
Blush'd at the praise of their own loveliness;
And there were sudden partings, such as press
The life from out young hearts, and choking sighs
Which ne'er might be repeated: who could guess
If ever more should meet those mutual eyes,
Since upon night so sweet such awful morn could rise!

And there was mounting in hot haste: the steed,
The mustering squadron, and the clattering car,
Went pouring forward with impetuous speed,
And swiftly forming in the ranks of war;
And the deep thunder peal on peal afar;
And near, the beat of the alarming drum
Roused up the soldier ere the morning star;
While throng'd the citizens with terror dumb,
Or whispering with white lips—"The foe!
      They come! they come!"

Last noon beheld them full of lusty life,
Last eve in Beauty's circle proudly gay;
The midnight brought the signal sound of strife,
The morn the marshalling in arms,—the day

Battle's magnificently stern array!
The thunder-clouds close o'er it, which when rent,
The earth is covered thick with other clay,
Which her own clay shall cover, heaped and pent,
Rider and horse,—friend, foe,—in one red burial blent!

THE CHARGE OF THE LIGHT BRIGADE

ALFRED TENNYSON

A mistaken order at Balaklava in the Crimean War of 1854 led to the mowing down of a great part of a gallant English brigade which obeyed the order in the face of the Russian guns. The last survivor of the famous light brigade died in London in 1923 at the age of ninety-one.

Half a league, half a league,
Half a league onward,
All in the valley of Death
    Rode the six hundred.
"Forward, the Light Brigade!
Charge for the guns!" he said:
Into the valley of Death
    Rode the six hundred.

"Forward, the Light Brigade!"
Was there a man dismayed?
Not tho' the soldier knew
    Some one had blundered:
Theirs not to make reply,
Theirs not to reason why,
Theirs but to do and die:
Into the valley of Death
    Rode the six hundred.

Cannon to right of them,
Cannon to left of them,
Cannon in front of them
   Volleyed and thundered;
Storm'd at with shot and shell,
Boldly they rode and well,
Into the jaws of Death,
Into the mouth of Hell,
   Rode the six hundred.

Flashed all their sabres bare,
Flashed as they turned in air,
Sab'ring the gunners there,
Charging an army, while
   All the world wondered:
Plunged in the battery smoke,
Right thro' the line they broke,
Cossack and Russian
Reel'd from the sabre-stroke,
   Shatter'd and sundered.
Then they rode back, but not—
   Not the six hundred.

Cannon to right of them,
Cannon to left of them,
Cannon behind them
   Volleyed and thundered:
Stormed at with shot and shell,
While horse and hero fell,
They that had fought so well
Came through the jaws of death
Back from the mouth of hell,
All that was left of them—
   Left of six hundred.

When can their glory fade?
Oh, the wild charge they made!
All the world wondered.
Honor the charge they made!
Honor the Light Brigade—
Noble six hundred!

BREATHES THERE THE MAN

WALTER SCOTT

From *"The Lay of the Last Minstrel"*

Breathes there the man with soul so dead
Who never to himself hath said:
  "This is my own, my native land?"
Whose heart hath ne'er within him burned
As home his footsteps he hath turned,
  From wandering on a foreign strand?
If such there breathe, go mark him well;
For him no minstrel raptures swell;
High though his titles, proud his name,
Boundless his wealth as wish can claim,
Despite those titles, power and pelf,
The wretch concentred all in self,
Living, shall forfeit fair renown,
And, doubly dying, shall go down
To the vile dust from whence he sprung,
Unwept, unhonored, and unsung.

OLD IRONSIDES

OLIVER WENDELL HOLMES

In 1830, when Oliver Wendell Holmes was a law student at Harvard, he read one day in a Boston paper of the proposed demolition of the historic U.S. frigate, Constitution, *then become old and useless. His patriotic indignation aroused, he dashed off the lines of this poem and a day or so later it was printed in the paper. The instant popular attention it excited resulted in the preservation of the ship.*

Ay, tear her tattered ensign down!
  Long has it waved on high,
And many an eye has danced to see
  That banner in the sky;
Beneath it rung the battle shout,
  And burst the cannon's roar;—
The meteor of the ocean air
  Shall sweep the clouds no more.

Her deck, once red with heroes' blood,
  Where knelt the vanquished foe,
Where winds were hurrying o'er the flood,
  And waves were white below.
No more shall feel the victor's tread,
  Or know the conquered knee;
The harpies of the shore shall pluck
  The eagle of the sea!

O, better that her shattered hulk
  Should sink beneath the wave;
Her thunders shook the mighty deep,
  And there should be her grave;
Nail to the mast her holy flag,
  Set every threadbare sail,
And give her to the god of storms,
  The lightning and the gale!

PAUL REVERE'S RIDE

HENRY W. LONGFELLOW

Listen, my children, and you shall hear
Of the midnight ride of Paul Revere,
On the eighteenth of April, in Seventy-five;
Hardly a man is now alive
Who remembers that famous day and year.

He said to his friend, "If the British march
By land or sea from the town to-night,
Hang a lantern aloft in the belfry arch
Of the North Church tower as a signal light,—
One if by land, and two if by sea;
And I on the opposite shore will be,
Ready to ride and spread the alarm
Through every Middlesex village and farm,
For the country folk to be up and to arm."

Then he said "Good-night!" and with muffled **oar**
Silently rowed to the Charlestown shore,
Just as the moon rose over the bay,
Where swinging wide at her moorings lay
The *Somerset,* British man-of-war;
A phantom ship, with each mast and spar
Across the moon like a prison bar,
And a huge black hulk, that was magnified
By its own reflection in the tide.

Meanwhile, his friend through alley and **street**
Wanders and watches, with eager ears,
Till in the silence around him he hears
The muster of men at the barrack door,
The sound of arms, and the tramp of feet,

And the measured tread of the grenadiers,
Marching down to their boats on the shore.

Then he climbed the tower of the Old North Church,
By the wooden stairs, with stealthy tread,
To the belfry chamber overhead,
And startled the pigeons from their perch
On the sombre rafters, that round him made
Masses and moving shapes of shade,—
By the trembling ladder, steep and tall,
To the highest window in the wall,
Where he paused to listen and look down
A moment on the roofs of the town
And the moonlight flowing over all.

Beneath, in the churchyard, lay the dead,
In their night encampment on the hill,
Wrapped in silence so deep and still
That he could hear, like a sentinel's tread,
The watchful night-wind, as it went
Creeping along from tent to tent,
And seeming to whisper, "All is well!"
A moment only he feels the spell
Of the place and the hour, and the secret dread
Of the lonely belfry and the dead;
For suddenly all his thoughts are bent
On a shadowy something far away,
Where the river widens to meet the bay,—
A line of black that bends and floats
On the rising tide like a bridge of boats.

Meanwhile, impatient to mount and ride,
Booted and spurred, with a heavy stride
On the opposite shore walked Paul Revere.
Now he patted his horse's side,

Now he gazed at the landscape far and near,
Then, impetuous, stamped the earth,
And turned and tightened his saddle girth;
But mostly he watched with eager search
The belfry tower of the Old North Church,
As it rose above the graves on the hill,
Lonely and spectral and sombre and still.
And lo! as he looks, on the belfry's height
A glimmer, and then a gleam of light!
He springs to the saddle, the bridle he turns,
But lingers and gazes, till full on his sight
A second lamp in the belfry burns.

A hurry of hoofs in a village street,
A shape in the moonlight, a bulk in the dark,
And beneath, from the pebbles, in passing, a spark
Struck out by a steed flying fearless and fleet;
That was all! And yet, through the gloom and the light,
The fate of a nation was riding that night;
And the spark struck out by that steed, in his flight,
Kindled the land into flame with its heat.
He has left the village and mounted the steep,
And beneath him, tranquil and broad and deep,
Is the Mystic, meeting the ocean tides;
And under the alders that skirt its edge,
Now soft on the sand, now loud on the ledge,
Is heard the tramp of his steed as he rides.

It was twelve by the village clock
When he crossed the bridge into Medford town.
He heard the crowing of the cock
And the barking of the farmer's dog,
And felt the damp of the river fog,
That rises after the sun goes down.

It was one by the village clock,
When he galloped into Lexington.
He saw the gilded weathercock
Swim in the moonlight as he passed,
And the meeting-house windows, blank and bare,
Gaze at him with a spectral glare,
As if they already stood aghast
At the bloody work they would look upon.

It was two by the village clock,
When he came to the bridge in Concord town.
He heard the bleating of the flock,
And the twitter of birds among the trees,
And felt the breath of the morning breeze
Blowing over the meadow brown.
And one was safe and asleep in his bed
Who at the bridge would be first to fall,
Who that day would be lying dead,
Pierced by a British musket ball.

You know the rest. In the books you have read,
How the British Regulars fired and fled,—
How the farmers gave them ball for ball,
From behind each fence and farmyard wall,
Chasing the redcoats down the lane,
Then crossing the fields to emerge again
Under the trees at the turn of the road,
And only pausing to fire and load.

So through the night rode Paul Revere;
And so through the night went his cry of alarm
To every Middlesex village and farm,—
A cry of defiance, and not of fear,
A voice in the darkness, a knock at the door,

And a word that shall echo for evermore!
For, borne on the night-wind of the Past,
Through all our history, to the last,
In the hour of darkness and peril and need,
The people will waken and listen to hear
The hurrying hoof-beats of that steed,
And the midnight message of Paul Revere.

CONCORD HYMN

RALPH WALDO EMERSON

By the rude bridge that arched the flood,
    Their flag to April's breeze unfurled,
Here once the embattled farmers stood,
    And fired the shot heard round the world.

The foe long since in silence slept;
    Alike the conqueror silent sleeps;
And Time the ruined bridge has swept
    Down the dark stream which seaward creeps.

On this green bank, by this soft stream,
    We set today a votive stone;
That memory may their deed redeem,
    When, like our sires, our sons are gone.

Spirit, that made those spirits dare
    To die, and leave their children free,
Bid Time and Nature gently spare
    The shaft we raise to them and thee.

Emerson lived for many years in Concord, not far from the famous bridge where the Minute-men took their stand on April 19, 1775. He made this hymn to be sung at the dedication of the Battle Monument which took place on April 19, 1836.

THE STAR-SPANGLED BANNER

FRANCIS SCOTT KEY

O! say, can you see, by the dawn's early light,
 What so proudly we hailed at the twilight's last gleam-
  ing—
Whose broad stripes and bright stars, through the perilous
  fight,
 O'er the ramparts we watched were so gallantly stream-
  ing!
And the rocket's red glare, the bombs bursting in air,
Gave proof through the night that our flag was still there;
O! say, does that star-spangled banner yet wave
O'er the land of the free, and the home of the brave?

On that shore dimly seen through the mists of the deep,
 Where the foe's haughty host in dread silence reposes,
What is that which the breeze, o'er the towering steep,
 As it fitfully blows, half conceals, half discloses?
Now it catches the gleam of the morning's first beam,
In full glory reflected now shines on the stream;
'Tis the star-spangled banner; O long may it wave
O'er the land of the free, and the home of the brave!

And where is that band who so vauntingly swore
 That the havoc of war and the battle's confusion
A home and a country should leave us no more?
 Their blood has washed out their foul footsteps' pollution.
No refuge could save the hireling and slave
From the terror of flight, or the gloom of the grave;
And the star-spangled banner in triumph doth wave
O'er the land of the free, and the home of the brave.

O! thus be it ever, when freemen shall stand
  Between their loved homes and wild war's desolation!
Blest with victory and peace, may the heav'n-rescued land
  Praise the power that hath made and preserved us a
    nation.
Then conquer we must, for our cause it is just,
And this be our motto—"In God is our trust":
And the star-spangled banner in triumph shall wave
O'er the land of the free, and the home of the brave.

Howard R. Driggs, during his years as Professor of History at New York University, taught his students that Americans should not sing only the first verse of doubt in our national anthem, but go on always to the verses of confidence and victory.

When the British troops invaded Washington in 1814, Francis Key, a young Washington lawyer, was sent by President Madison to the British General to negotiate for the release of an American prisoner. Key was himself held, because the British were preparing to attack Fort Henry. He watched the bombardment through the night from the deck of a ship. The American flag remained flying over the fort and at dawn Key wrote this great patriotic poem.

THE FLAG GOES BY

HENRY HOLCOMB BENNETT

Hats off!
Along the street there comes
A blare of bugles, a ruffle of drums,
A flash of color beneath the sky:
Hats off!
The flag is passing by!

  Blue and crimson and white it shines,
Over the steel-tipped, ordered lines.
Hats off!

The colors before us fly;
But more than the flag is passing by.

Sea-fights and land-fights, grim and great,
Fought to make and to save the State:
Weary marches and sinking ships;
Cheers of victory on dying lips;

Days of plenty and years of peace;
March of a strong land's swift increase;
Equal justice, right and law,
Stately honor and reverend awe;

Sign of a nation, great and strong
To ward her people from foreign wrong:
Pride and glory and honor,—all
Live in the colors to stand or fall.

Hats off!
Along the street there comes
A blare of bugles, a ruffle of drums;
And loyal hearts are beating high:
Hats off!
The flag is passing by!

BARBARA FRIETCHIE

JOHN GREENLEAF WHITTIER

Up from the meadows rich with corn,
Clear in the cool September morn,

The clustered spires of Frederick stand
Green-walled by the hills of Maryland.

Round about them orchards sweep,
Apple and peach tree fruited deep,

Fair as the garden of the Lord
To the eyes of the famished rebel horde,

On that pleasant morn of the early fall
When Lee marched over the mountain-wall,—

Over the mountains winding down,
Horse and foot, into Frederick town.

Forty flags with their silver stars,
Forty flags with their crimson bars,

Flapped in the morning wind: the sun
Of noon looked down, and saw not one.

Up rose old Barbara Frietchie then,
Bowed with her fourscore years and ten,

Bravest of all in Frederick town,
She took up the flag the men hauled down.

In her attic window the staff she set,
To show that one heart was loyal yet.

Up the street came the rebel tread,
Stonewall Jackson riding ahead.

Under his slouched hat left and right
He glanced: the old flag met his sight.

"Halt!"—the dust-brown ranks stood fast
"Fire!"—out blazed the rifle-blast.

It shivered the window, pane and sash;
It rent the banner with seam and gash.

Quick, as it fell, from the broken staff
Dame Barbara snatched the silken scarf.

She leaned far out on the window-sill,
And shook it forth with a royal will.

"Shoot, if you must, this old gray head,
But spare your country's flag," she said.

A shade of sadness, a blush of shame,
Over the face of the leader came;

The nobler nature within him stirred
To life at that woman's deed and word:

"Who touches a hair of yon gray head
Dies like a dog! March on!" he said.

All day long through Frederick street
Sounded the tread of marching feet;

All day long that free flag toss'd
Over the heads of the rebel host.

Ever its torn folds rose and fell
On the loyal winds that loved it well;

And through the hill-gaps sunset light
Shone over it with a warm good-night.

Barbara Frietchie's work is o'er,
And the rebel rides on his raids no more.

Honor to her! and let a tear
Fall, for her sake, on Stonewall's bier.

Over Barbara Frietchie's grave,
Flag of freedom and union wave!

Peace and order and beauty draw
Round thy symbol of light and law;

And ever the stars above look down
On thy stars below in Frederick town.

SHERIDAN'S RIDE

T. BUCHANAN READ

Sheridan, returning from official business at Washington, slept at Winchester on the night of October 18, 1864. Early next morning he heard sounds of bombardment and knew that an attack must have been made by the Confederate Army. He mounted his horse and started for the field, reaching there just in time to rally the Union forces and turn defeat into a decisive victory.

Up from the South at break of day,
Bringing to Winchester fresh dismay,
The affrighted air with a shudder bore,
Like a herald in haste, to the chieftain's door,
The terrible grumble, and rumble, and roar,
Telling the battle was on once more,
And Sheridan twenty miles away.

And wider still those billows of war
Thundered along the horizon's bar;
And louder yet into Winchester rolled

The roar of that red sea uncontrolled,
Making the blood of the listener cold
As he thought of the stake in that fiery fray,
And Sheridan twenty miles away.

But there is a road from Winchester town,
A good, broad highway leading down;
And there, through the flush of the morning light,
A steed as black as the steeds of night
Was seen to pass as with eagle flight;
As if he knew the terrible need,
He stretched away with his utmost speed;
Hills rose and fell; but his heart was gay,
With Sheridan fifteen miles away.

Still sprung from those swift hoofs, thundering South,
The dust, like smoke from the cannon's mouth;
Or the trail of a comet, sweeping faster and faster,
Foreboding to traitors the doom of disaster.
The heart of the steed and the heart of the master
Were beating like prisoners assaulting their walls,
Impatient to be where the battle-field calls;
Every nerve of the charger was strained to full play,
With Sheridan only ten miles away.

Under his spurning feet the road
Like an arrowy Alpine river flowed.
And the landscape sped away behind
Like an ocean flying before the wind,
And the steed, like a barque fed with furnace ire,
Swept on, with his wild eye full of fire.
But lo! he is nearing his heart's desire;
He is snuffing the smoke of the roaring fray,
With Sheridan only five miles away.

The first that the general saw were the groups
Of stragglers, and then the retreating troops;
What was done? What to do? A glance told him both.
Then, striking his spurs, with a terrible oath,
He dashed down the line 'mid a storm of huzzas,
And the wave of retreat checked its course there, because
The sight of the master compelled it to pause.
With foam and with dust the black charger was gray;
By the flash of his eye, and the red nostril's play,
He seemed to the whole great army to say,
"I have brought you Sheridan all the way
From Winchester down to save the day!"

Hurrah! Hurrah for Sheridan!
Hurrah! Hurrah for horse and man!
And when their statues are placed on high,
Under the dome of the Union sky,
The American soldier's Temple of Fame;
There with the glorious general's name,
Be it said, in letters both bold and bright,
    "Here is the steed that saved the day,
By carrying Sheridan into the fight,
    From Winchester, twenty miles away!"

KILLED AT THE FORD

HENRY W. LONGFELLOW

He is dead, the beautiful youth,
The heart of honor, the tongue of truth,
He, the life and light of us all,
Whose voice was blithe as a bugle call,
Whom all eyes followed with one consent,
The cheer of whose laugh, and whose pleasant word,
Hushed all murmurs of discontent.

Only last night as we rode along,
Down the dark of the mountain gap,
To visit the picket-guard at the ford,
Little dreaming of any mishap,
He was humming the words of some old song:
"Two red roses he had on his cap,
And another he bore at the point of his sword."

Sudden and swift a whistling ball
Came out of a wood and the voice was still;
Something I heard in the darkness fall,
And for a moment my blood grew chill;
I spoke in a whisper as one who speaks
In a room where some one is lying dead;
But he made no answer to what I said.

We lifted him up to his saddle again,
And through the mire and the mist and the rain
Carried him back to the silent camp,
And laid him as if asleep on his bed;
And I saw by the light of the surgeon's lamp
Two white roses upon his cheeks
And one, just over his heart, blood-red!

And I saw in a vision how far and fleet
That fatal bullet went speeding forth,
Till it reached a town in the distant North,
Till it reached a house in a sunny street,
Till it reached a heart that ceased to beat
Without a murmur, without a cry;
And a bell was tolled in that far-off town
For one who had passed from cross to crown,
And the neighbors wondered that she should die.

THE REVENGE OF RAIN-IN-THE-FACE

HENRY W. LONGFELLOW

In 1876 it was found necessary to transfer the Sioux Indians from one reservation to another, but the Indians refused to go. Lt. Col. George A. Custer was sent to make them obey, and a fight ensued during which Custer and all his men were killed. Longfellow's story of the fight emphasizes the Indian leader, Rain-in-the-Face, who had been arrested some months before by Capt. Tom Custer and had vowed to eat the Captain's heart. It is said that he made good his threat, but Col. George Custer was not thus mutilated.

In that desolate land and lone,
Where the Big Horn and Yellowstone
   Roar down their mountain path,
By their fires the Sioux Chiefs
Muttered their woes and griefs
   And the menace of their wrath.

"Revenge!" cried Rain-in-the-Face,
"Revenge upon all the race
   Of the white Chief with yellow hair!"
And the mountains dark and high
From their crags re-echoed the cry
   Of his anger and despair.

In the meadow, spreading wide
By woodland and riverside
   The Indian village stood;
All was silent as a dream,
Save the rushing of the stream
   And the blue-jay in the wood.

In his war paint and his beads,
Like a bison among the reeds,
 In ambush the Sitting Bull
Lay with three thousand braves
Crouched in the clefts and caves,
 Savage, unmerciful!

Into the fatal snare
The White Chief with yellow hair
 And his three hundred men
Dashed headlong, sword in hand;
But of that gallant band
 Not one returned again.

The sudden darkness of death
Overwhelmed them like the breath
 And smoke of a furnace fire:
By the river's bank, and between
The rocks of the ravine,
 They lay in their bloody attire.

But the foemen fled in the night,
And Rain-in-the-Face, in his flight,
 Uplifted high in air
As a ghastly trophy, bore
The brave heart, that beat no more,
 Of the White Chief with yellow hair.

Whose was the right and the wrong?
Sing it, O funeral song,
 With a voice that is full of tears,
And say that our broken faith
Wrought all this ruin and scathe,
 In the Year of a Hundred Years.

ATLANTIC CHARTER: 1942

FRANCIS BRETT YOUNG

What were you carrying, Pilgrims, Pilgrims?
What did you carry beyond the sea?
> *We carried the Book, we carried the Sword,*
> A steadfast heart in the fear of the Lord,
> And a living faith in His plighted word
> *That all men should be free.*

What were your memories, Pilgrims, Pilgrims?
What of the dreams you bore away?
> We carried the songs our fathers sung
> By the hearths of home when they were young,
> And the comely words of the mother-tongue
> In which they learnt to pray.

What did you find there, Pilgrims, Pilgrims?
What did you find beyond the waves?
> A stubborn land and a barren shore,
> Hunger and want and sickness sore:
> All these we found and gladly bore
> Rather than be slaves.

How did you fare there, Pilgrims, Pilgrims?
What did you build in that stubborn land?
> We felled the forest and tilled the sod
> Of a continent no man had trod
> And we stablished there, in the Grace of God,
> The rights whereby we stand.

What are you bringing us, Pilgrims, Pilgrims?
Bringing us back in this bitter day?

The selfsame things we carried away:
The Book, the Sword,
The fear of the Lord,
And the boons our fathers dearly bought:
Freedom of Worship, Speech and Thought,
Freedom from Want, Freedom from Fear,
The liberties we hold most dear,
And who shall say us Nay?

From *The Island*

THE COMING AMERICAN

SAM WALTER FOSS

Bring me men to match my mountains,
Bring me men to match my plains,
And new eras in their brains.
Bring me men to match my prairies,
Men to match my inland seas,
Men whose thoughts shall pave a highway
Up to ampler destinies,
Pioneers to cleanse thought's marshlands,
    And to cleanse old error's fen;
Bring me men to match my mountains—
    Bring me men!

Bring me men to match my forests,
Strong to fight the storm and beast,
Branching toward the skyey future,
Rooted on the futile past.
Bring me men to match my valleys,
    Tolerant of rain and snow,
Men within whose fruitful purpose

Time's consummate blooms shall grow,
Men to tame the tigerish instincts
    Of the lair and cave and den,
Cleanse the dragon slime of nature—
    Bring me men!

Bring me men to match my rivers,
    Continent cleansers, flowing free,
Drawn by eternal madness,
    To be mingled with the sea—
Men of oceanic impulse,
    Men whose moral currents sweep
Toward the wide, infolding ocean
    Of an undiscovered deep—
Men who feel the strong pulsation
    Of the central sea, and then
Time their currents by its earth throbs—
    Bring me Men.

SOLDIER, WHAT DID YOU SEE?

DON BLANDING

What did you see, Soldier? What did you see at war?
I saw such glory and horror as I've never seen before.
I saw men's hearts burned naked in red crucibles of pain.
I saw such godlike courage as I'll never see again.

What did you hear, Soldier? What did you hear at war?
I heard the prayers on lips of men who had never prayed be-
    fore.
I heard men tell their very souls, confessing each dark stain.
I heard men speak the sacred things they will not speak again.

What did you eat, Soldier? What did you eat at war?
I ate the sour bread of fear, the acrid salt of gore.
My lips were burned with wine of hate, the scalding drink of
    Cain.
My tongue has known a bitter taste I would not taste again.

What did you think, Soldier? What did you think at war?
I thought, how strange we have not learned from wars that
    raged before,
Except new ways of killing, new multiples of pain.
Is all the blood that men have shed but blood shed all in vain?

What did you learn, Soldier? What did you learn at war?
I learned that we must learn sometime what was not learned
    before,
That victories won on battlefields are victories won in vain
Unless in peace we kill the germs that breed new wars again.

What did you pray, Soldier? What did you pray at war?
I prayed that we might do the thing we have not done before;
That we might mobilize for peace . . . nor mobilize in vain.
Lest Christ and man be forced to climb stark Calvary again.

GRASS

CARL SANDBURG

Pile the bodies high at Austerlitz and Waterloo.
Shovel them under and let me work—
      I am the grass; I cover all.
And pile them high at Gettysburg
And pile them high at Ypres and Verdun.
Shovel them under and let me work.
Two years, ten years, and passengers ask the conductor:
      What place is this?
      Where are we now?
      Let me work.
      I am the grass.

Part Four

SONGS OF LIFE

A thing of beauty is a joy for ever:
Its loveliness increases; it will never
Pass into nothingness; but still will keep
A bower quiet for us, and a sleep
Full of sweet dreams, and health, and quiet breathing.
                              From ENDYMION, John Keats

IF

RUDYARD KIPLING

If you can keep your head when all about you
    Are losing theirs and blaming it on you,
If you can trust yourself when all men doubt you,
    But make allowance for their doubting too;
If you can wait and not be tired by waiting,
    Or being lied about, don't deal in lies,
Or being hated, don't give way to hating,
    And yet don't look too good, or talk too wise:

If you can dream—and not make dreams your master;
    If you can think—and not make thoughts your aim,
If you can meet with Triumph and Disaster
    And treat those two impostors just the same;
If you can bear to hear the truth you've spoken
    Twisted by knaves to make a trap for fools,
Or watch the things you gave your life to, broken,
    And stoop and build 'em up with worn-out tools:

If you can make one heap of all your winnings;
    And risk it on one turn of pitch-and-toss,
And lose, and start again at your beginnings
    And never breathe a word about your loss;
If you can force your heart and nerve and sinew
    To serve your turn long after they are gone
And so hold on when there is nothing in you
    Except the Will which says to them: "Hold on!"

If you can talk with crowds and keep your virtue,
    Or walk with Kings—nor lose the common touch,
If neither foes nor loving friends can hurt you,
    If all men count with you, but none too much;

If

If you can fill the unforgiving minute
  With sixty seconds' worth of distance run,
Yours is the Earth and everything that's in it,
  And—which is more—you'll be a Man, my son!

This poem, written in 1910, remains a steady favorite with men. It came out on top recently in a popular vote at Yale University.

FOUR THINGS

HENRY VAN DYKE

Four things a man must learn to do
If he would make his record true;
To think without confusion clearly,
To love his fellow-men sincerely;
To act from honest motives purely;
To trust in God and Heaven securely.

OPPORTUNITY

EDWARD ROWLAND SILL

This I beheld, or dreamed it in a dream:—
There spread a cloud of dust along a plain;
And underneath the cloud, or in it, raged
A furious battle, and men yelled, and swords
Shocked upon swords and shields. A prince's banner
Wavered, then staggered backward, hemmed by foes.
A craven hung along the battle's edge,
And thought, "Had I a sword of keener steel—
That blue blade that the king's son bears,—but this

Blunt thing!" he snapt and flung it from his hand,
And lowering crept away and left the field.
Then came the king's son, wounded, sore bestead,
And weaponless, and saw the broken sword,
Hilt-buried in the dry and trodden sand,
And ran and snatched it, and with battle-shout
Lifted afresh he hewed his enemy down,
And saved a great cause that heroic day.

PANDORA'S SONG

WILLIAM VAUGHN MOODY

Of wounds and sore defeat
I made my battle stay;
Wingèd sandals for my feet
I wove of my delay;
Of weariness and fear
I made my shouting spear;
Of loss and doubt and dread
And swift oncoming doom
I made a helmet for my head
And a floating plume.
From the shutting mist of death
And the failure of the breath,
I made a battle horn to blow
Across the vales of overthrow.
O hearken, love, the battle horn!
The triumph clear, the silver scorn!
O hearken where the echoes bring
Down the grey disastrous morn
Laughter and rallying!

From Moody's poetic drama, "The Fire-bringer."

THE CELESTIAL SURGEON

ROBERT LOUIS STEVENSON

If I have faltered more or less
My great task of happiness;
If I have moved among my race
And shown no glorious morning face;
If beams from happy human eyes
Have moved me not; if morning skies,
Books, and my food, and summer rain
Knocked on my sullen heart in vain,
Lord, Thy most pointed pleasure take,
And stab my spirit broad awake;
Or, Lord, if too obdurate I,
Choose Thou, before that spirit die,
A piercing pain, a killing sin,
And to my dead heart run them in!

INVICTUS

WILLIAM ERNEST HENLEY

Out of the night that covers me,
  Black as the Pit from pole to pole,
I thank whatever gods may be
  For my unconquerable soul.

In the fell clutch of circumstance
  I have not winced nor cried aloud.
Under the bludgeonings of chance
  My head is bloody, but unbowed.

Beyond this place of wrath and tears
  Looms but the horror of the shade,
And yet the menace of the years
  Finds, and shall find me, unafraid.

It matters not how strait the gate,
  How charged with punishments the scroll,
I am the master of my fate;
  I am the captain of my soul.

When he was a boy of twelve Henley became a cripple, but he fought his disadvantage bravely all his life, with his head "unbowed." He met Robert Louis Stevenson in a hospital in Edinburgh and the two became great friends. Stevenson used Henley as a model for Long John Silver in "Treasure Island."

RABBI BEN EZRA

ROBERT BROWNING

Grow old along with me!
The best is yet to be,
The last of life, for which the first was made:
Our times are in his hand
Who saith, "A whole I planned,
Youth shows but half; trust God: see all, nor be afraid!"

Not that, amassing flowers,
Youth sighed, "Which rose make ours,
Which lily leave and then as best recall?"
Not that, admiring stars,
It yearned, "Nor Jove, nor Mars;
Mine be some figured flame which blends, transcends them
    all!"

Rabbi Ben Ezra

Not for such hopes and fears
Annulling youth's brief years,
Do I remonstrate: folly wide the mark!
Rather I prize the doubt
Low kinds exist without,
Finished and finite clods, untroubled by a spark.

. . . .

Then, welcome each rebuff
That turns earth's smoothness rough,
Each sting that bids nor sit nor stand but go!
Be our joys three-parts pain!
Strive, and hold cheap the strain;
Learn, nor account the pang; dare, never grudge the throe!

For thence,—a paradox
Which comforts while it mocks,—
Life shall succeed in that it seems to fail:
What I aspired to be,
And was not, comforts me;
A brute I might have been, but would not sink i' the scale.

What is he but a brute
Whose flesh has soul to suit,
Whose spirit works lest arms and legs want play?
To man propose this test—
Thy body at its best,
How far can that project thy soul on its lone way?

. . . .

For pleasant is this flesh;
Our soul, in its rose-mesh
Pulled ever to the earth, still yearns for rest:
Would we some prize might hold
To match those manifold
Possessions of the brute—gain most as we did best!

Let us not always say,
"Spite of this flesh today
I strove, made head, gained ground upon the whole!"
As the bird wings and sings,
Let us cry, "All good things
Are ours, nor soul helps flesh more, now, than flesh helps
    soul!"

Therefore I summon age
To grant youth's heritage,
Life's struggle having so far reached its term:
Thence shall I pass, approved
A man, for aye removed
From the developed brute; a god, though in the germ.

  · · · · · · · · ·

For note, when evening shuts,
A certain moment cuts
The deed off, calls the glory from the grey:
A whisper from the west
Shoots—"Add this to the rest,
Take it and try its worth: here dies another day."

  · · · · · · · · ·

Not on the vulgar mass
Called "work," must sentence pass,
Things done, that took the eye and had the price;
O'er which, from level stand,
The low world laid its hand,
Found straightway to its mind, could value in a trice:

But all, the world's coarse thumb
And finger failed to plumb,
So passed in making up the main account;
All instincts immature,
All purposes unsure,

That weighed not as his work, yet swelled the man's amount:

Thoughts hardly to be packed
Into a narrow act,
Fancies that broke through language and escaped;
All I could never be,
All, men ignored in me,
This, I was worth to God, whose wheel the pitcher shaped.

Ay, note that Potter's wheel,
That metaphor! and feel
Why time spins fast, why passive lies our clay,—
Thou, to whom fools propound,
When the wine makes its round,
"Since life fleets, all is change; the Past gone, seize today!"

Fool! All that is, at all,
Lasts ever, past recall;
Earth changes, but thy soul and God stand sure:
What entered into thee,
That was, is, and shall be:
Time's wheel runs back or stops: Potter and clay endure.

. . . .

Look thou not down but up!
To uses of a cup,
The festal board, lamp's flash and trumpet's peal,
The new wine's flaming flow,
The Master's lips aglow!
Thou, Heaven's consummate cup, what needst thou with
     earth's wheel?

But I need, now as then,
Thee, God, who mouldest men,
And since, now even while the whirl was worst,
Did I—to the wheel of life

With shapes and colors rife,
Bound dizzily—mistake my end, to slake my thirst:

So, take and use thy work,
Amend what flaws may lurk,
What strain o' the stuff, what warpings past the aim!
My times be in thy hand!
Perfect the cup as planned!
Let age approve of youth, and death complete the same!

PROSPICE

ROBERT BROWNING

Fear death?—to feel the fog in my throat,
    The mist in my face,
When the snows begin, and the blasts denote
    I am nearing the place,
The power of the night, the press of the storm,
    The post of the foe;
Where he stands, the Arch Fear in a visible form,
    Yet the strong man must go:
For the journey is done and the summit attained,
    And the barriers fall,
Though a battle's to fight ere a guerdon be gained,
    The reward of it all.
I was ever a fighter, so—one fight more,
    The best and the last!
I would hate that death bandaged my eyes, and forbore,
    And bade me creep past.
No! let me taste the whole of it, fare like my peers
    The heroes of old,
Bear the brunt, in a minute pay glad life's arrears
    Of pain, darkness, and cold.

For sudden the worst turns the best to the brave,
 The black minute's at end.
And the elements' rage, the fiend-voices that rave
 Shall dwindle, shall blend,
Shall change, shall become first a peace out of pain,
 Then a light, then thy breast,
O thou soul of my soul! I shall clasp thee again,
 And with God be the rest!

FATE

SUSAN MARR SPALDING

Two shall be born, the whole wide world apart,
And speak in different tongues and have no thought
Each of the other's being, and no heed;
And these, o'er unknown seas, to unknown lands
Shall cross, escaping wreck, defying death;
And all unconsciously shape every act
And bend each wandering step to this one end—
That one day out of darkness they shall meet
And read life's meaning in each other's eyes.

And two shall walk some narrow way of life
So nearly side by side that, should one turn
Ever so little space to left or right,
They needs must stand acknowledged, face to face,
And yet, with wistful eyes that never meet,
And groping hands that never clasp, and lips
Calling in vain to ears that never hear,
They seek each other all their weary days
And die unsatisfied—and this is Fate!

AT THE CROSSROADS

RICHARD HOVEY

You to the left and I to the right,
For the ways of men must sever—
And it well may be for a day and a night,
And it well may be forever.
But whether we meet or whether we part
(For our ways are past our knowing)
A pledge from the heart to its fellow heart
On the ways we all are going!
Here's luck!
For we know not where we are going.

Whether we win or whether we lose
With the hands that life is dealing,
It is not we nor the ways we choose
But the fall of the cards that's sealing.
There's a fate in love and a fate in fight,
And the best of us all go under—
And whether we're wrong or whether we're right,
We win, sometimes to our wonder.
Here's luck!
That we may not yet go under.

With a steady swing and an open brow
We have tramped the ways together,
But we're clasping hands at the crossroads now
In the Fiend's own night for weather;
And whether we bleed or whether we smile
In the leagues that lie before us,
The ways of life are many a mile

And the dark of Fate is o'er us.
Here's luck!
And a cheer for the dark before us!

You to the left and I to the right,
For the ways of men must sever,
And it well may be for a day and a night
And it well may be forever!
But whether we live or whether we die
(For the end is past our knowing),
Here's two frank hearts and an open sky,
Be a fair or ill wind blowing!
Here's luck!
In the teeth of all winds blowing.

THOUGH HE THAT EVER KIND AND TRUE

ROBERT LOUIS STEVENSON

Though he that ever kind and true,
Kept stoutly step by step with you
Your whole long gusty lifetime through
        Be gone awhile before,
Be now, a moment gone before,
Yet doubt not, soon the seasons shall restore
        Your friend to you.

He has but turned a corner—still
He pushes on with right good will
Through mire and marsh, by heugh and hill
        That self-same arduous way,
That self-same, upland hopeful way
That you and he through many a doubtful day
        Attempted still.

He is not dead, this friend—not dead,
But in the path we mortals tread
Got some few trifling steps ahead,
      And nearer to the end
So that you too, once past the bend
Shall meet again, as face to face, this friend
      You fancy dead.

Push gaily on, strong heart! The while
You travel forward, mile by mile
He loiters with a backward smile
      Till you can overtake
And strains his eyes to search his wake
Or, whistling, as he sees you through the brake,
      Waits on a stile.

REQUIEM

ROBERT LOUIS STEVENSON

Robert Louis Stevenson made these lines during his last illness at Samoa, his South Sea Island home. They are almost a miniature record of his active, courageous life of seeking after health. The lines are graven on his tomb at Samoa.

Under the wide and starry sky
      Dig the grave and let me lie,
Glad did I live and gladly die,
      And I laid me down with a will.

This be the verse you grave for me:
      Here he lies where he longed to be,
Home is the sailor, home from sea,
      And the hunter home from the hill.

THE BREASTPLATE OF SAINT PATRICK

ANONYMOUS

I bind myself to-day
To the power of Heaven,
The light of sun,
The brightness of moon,
The splendor of fire,
The speed of lightning,
The swiftness of wind,
The depths of the sea,
The stability of the earth,
The firmness of rocks.

I bind myself to-day
To the power of God to guide me,
The might of God to uphold me,
The wisdom of God to teach me,
The eye of God to watch over me,
The ear of God to hear me,
The word of God to speak for me,
The hand of God to protect me,
The way of God to lie before me,
The shield of God to shelter me,
The host of God to defend me,
    Against the snares of demons,
    Against the temptations of vices,
    Against the lusts of nature,
    Against every man who meditates injury to me,
    Whether far or near,
    Alone, and in a multitude.

As someone has said, "What a lot of fine things this man Anonymous has written!"

THE TIGER

WILLIAM BLAKE

Tiger, tiger, burning bright
In the forests of the night!
What immortal hand or eye
Could frame thy fearful symmetry?

In what distant deeps or skies
Burnt the ardor of thine eyes?
On what wings dare he aspire—
What the hand dare seize the fire?

And what shoulder, and what art
Could twist the sinews of thy heart?
And when thy heart began to beat,
What dread hands and what dread **feet?**

What the hammer, what the chain,
In what furnace was thy brain?
What the anvil? What dread grasp
Dare its deadly terrors clasp?

When the stars threw down their spears,
And watered heaven with their tears,
Did he smile his work to see?
Did he who made the lamb make thee?

Tiger, tiger, burning bright
In the forests of the night,
What immortal hand or eye
Dare frame thy fearful symmetry?

IT IS NOT GROWING LIKE A TREE

BEN JONSON

It is not growing like a tree
In bulk, doth make Man better be;
Or standing long an oak, three hundred year,
To fall a log at last, dry, bald, and sere:
    A lily of a day
    Is fairer far in May,
Although it fall and die that night—
It was the plant and flower of Light.
In small proportions we just beauties see;
And in short measures life may perfect be.

MERCY

WILLIAM SHAKESPEARE

The quality of mercy is not strained;
It droppeth as the gentle rain from heaven
Upon the place beneath: it is twice blest,—
It blesseth him that gives and him that takes:
'Tis mightiest in the mightiest; it becomes
The thronèd monarch better than his crown:
His sceptre shows the force of temporal power,
The attribute to awe and majesty,
Wherein doth sit the dread and fear of kings;
But mercy is above this sceptred sway,—
It is enthronèd in the hearts of kings,
It is an attribute to God himself;
And earthly power doth then show likest God's,
When mercy seasons justice.

These lines from "The Merchant of Venice" are spoken by the girl-judge Portia in the court-room scene, when she is pleading with Shylock the Jew for mercy toward his victim.

TRUE LOVE

WILLIAM SHAKESPEARE

Let me not to the marriage of true minds
Admit impediments. Love is not love
Which alters when it alteration finds,
Or bends with the remover to remove:
O no! it is an ever-fixéd mark
That looks on tempests, and is never shaken;
It is the star to every wandering bark,
Whose worth 's unknown, although his height be taken.
Love's not Time's fool, though rosy lips and cheeks
Within his bending sickle's compass come;
Love alters not with his brief hours and weeks,
But bears it out ev'n to the edge of doom:—
    If this be error, and upon me proved,
    I never writ, nor no man ever loved.

POLONIUS' ADVICE TO LAERTES

WILLIAM SHAKESPEARE

*This is the advice a father gives to his son as he starts out from home
for college. It comes from Shakespeare's play about a young man—
"Hamlet."*

See thou character. Give thy thoughts no tongue,
Nor any unproportion'd thought his act.
Be thou familiar, but by no means vulgar:
The friends thou hast, and their adoption tried,
Grapple them to thy soul with hoops of steel;
But do not dull thy palm with entertainment
Of each new-hatch'd, unfledg'd comrade. Beware
Of entrance to a quarrel; but, being in,
Bear 't that th' opposed may beware of thee.
Give every man thine ear, but few thy voice:

Take each man's censure, but reserve thy judgment.
Costly thy habit as thy purse can buy,
But not express'd in fancy; rich, not gaudy:
For the apparel oft proclaims the man.
Neither a borrower nor a lender be;
For loan oft loses both itself and friend,
And borrowing dulls the edge of husbandry.
This above all: to thine own self be true;
And it must follow, as the night the day,
Thou canst not then be false to any man.

INGRATITUDE

WILLIAM SHAKESPEARE

Blow, blow, thou winter wind,
Thou art not so unkind
    As man's ingratitude;
Thy tooth is not so keen
Because thou art not seen,
    Although thy breath be rude.

Freeze, freeze, thou bitter sky,
Thou dost not bite so nigh
    As benefits forgot;
Though thou the waters warp,
Thy sting is not so sharp
    As friend remembered not.

From "As You Like It."

WHEN I WAS ONE-AND-TWENTY

A. E. HOUSMAN

When I was one-and-twenty
  I heard a wise man say,
"Give crowns and pounds and guineas
  But not your heart away;
Give pearls away and rubies
  But keep your fancy free."
But I was one-and-twenty,
  No use to talk to me.

When I was one-and-twenty
  I heard him say again,
"The heart out of the bosom
  Was never given in vain;
'Tis paid with sighs a plenty
  And sold for endless rue."
And I am two-and-twenty,
  And oh, 'tis true, 'tis true.

GIFTS

JAMES THOMSON

Give a man a horse he can ride,
  Give a man a boat he can sail;
And his rank and wealth, his strength and health,
  On sea nor shore shall fail.

Give a man a pipe he can smoke,
  Give a man a book he can read;
And his home is bright with a calm delight,
  Though the room be poor indeed.

Give a man a girl he can love,
    As I, O my love, love thee;
And his heart is great with the pulse of Fate,
    At home, on land, on sea.

I THINK I KNOW NO FINER THINGS THAN DOGS

HALLY CARRINGTON BRENT

Though prejudice perhaps my mind befogs,
I think I know no finer things than dogs:
The young ones, they of gay and bounding heart,
Who lure us in their games to take a part,
Who with mock tragedy their antics cloak
And, from their wild eyes' tail, admit the joke;
The old ones, with their wistful, fading eyes,
They who desire no further paradise
Than the warm comfort of a smile and hand,
Who tune their moods to ours and understand
Each word and gesture; they who lie and wait
To welcome us—with no rebuke if late.
Sublime the love they bear; but ask to live
Close to our feet, unrecompensed to give;
Beside which many men seem very logs—
I think I know no finer things than dogs.

BISHOP DOANE ON HIS DOG

GEORGE WASHINGTON DOANE

I am quite sure he thinks that I am God—
Since he is God on whom each one depends
For life, and all things that His bounty sends—
My dear old dog, most constant of all friends;
Not quick to mind, but quicker far than I
To Him whom God I know and own; his eye,
Deep brown and liquid, watches for my nod;
He is more patient underneath the rod
Than I, when God His wise corrections sends.
He looks love at me, deep as words e'er spake;
And from me never crumb nor sup will take
But he wags thanks with his most vocal tail;
And when some crashing noise wakes all his **fear,**
He is content and quiet, if I am near,
Secure that my protection will prevail.
So, faithful, mindful, thankful, trustful, he
Tells me what I unto my God should be.

THE BELLS

EDGAR ALLAN POE

Hear the sledges with the bells—
  Silver bells!
What a world of merriment their melody foretells!
  How they tinkle, tinkle, tinkle,
   In the icy air of night!
  While the stars, that oversprinkle
  All the heavens, seem to twinkle
   With a crystalline delight;
   Keeping time, time, time,

The Bells

          In a sort of Runic rhyme,
To the tintinnabulation that so musically **wells**
     From the bells, bells, bells, bells,
            Bells, bells, bells—
From the jingling and the tinkling of the bells.

          Hear the mellow wedding bells,
               Golden bells!
What a world of happiness their harmony foretells!
          Through the balmy air of night
          How they ring out their delight!
          From the molten-golden notes,
               And all in tune,
          What a liquid ditty floats
To the turtle dove that listens, while she gloats
               On the moon!
          Oh, from out the sounding cells,
What a gush of euphony voluminously wells!
               How it swells!
               How it dwells
          On the Future! how it tells
          Of the rapture that impels
     To the swinging and the ringing
          Of the bells, bells, bells,
     Of the bells, bells, bells, bells,
            Bells, bells, bells—
To the rhyming and the chiming of the bells!

          Hear the loud alarum bells—
               Brazen bells!
What a tale of terror now their turbulency tells!
          In the startled ear of night
          How they scream out their affright!
          Too much horrified to speak
          They can only shriek, shriek,
               Out of tune,

In a clamorous appealing to the mercy of the fire,
In a mad expostulation with the deaf and frantic fire,
  Leaping higher, higher, higher,
  With a desperate desire,
  And a resolute endeavor,
  Now—now to sit or never,
 By the side of the pale-faced moon.
  Oh, the bells, bells, bells!
  What a tale their terror tells
    Of despair!
  How they clang, and clash, and roar!
  What a horror they outpour
On the bosom of the palpitating air!
  Yet the ear it fully knows,
   By the twanging,
   And the clanging,
  How the danger ebbs and flows;
  Yet the ear distinctly tells,
   In the jangling,
   And the wrangling,
  How the danger sinks and swells,
By the sinking or the swelling in the anger of the bells—
   Of the bells—
  Of the bells, bells, bells, bells,
   Bells, bells, bells—
In the clamor and the clangor of the bells!

  Hear the tolling of the bells—
   Iron bells!
What a world of solemn thought their monody compels!
  In the silence of the night,
  How we shiver with affright
 At the melancholy menace of their tone!
  For every sound that floats
  From the rust within their throats
   Is a groan.

And the people—ah, the people—
They that dwell up in the steeple,
          All alone,
And who tolling, tolling, tolling,
    In that muffled monotone,
    Feel a glory in so rolling
    On the human heart a stone—
They are neither man nor woman—
They are neither brute or human—
          They are Ghouls:
And their king it is who tolls;
And he rolls, rolls, rolls,
          Rolls
    A pæan from the bells!
And his merry bosom swells
    With the pæan of the bells!
And he dances and he yells;
    Keeping time, time, time
        To the pæan of the bells—
          Of the bells:
Keeping time, time, time
In a sort of Runic rhyme,
    To the throbbing of the bells,
    Of the bells, bells, bells,—
        To the sobbing of the bells;
Keeping time, time, time,
    As he knells, knells, knells,
In a happy Runic rhyme
        To the rolling of the bells—
    Of the bells, bells, bells—
        To the tolling of the bells,
    Of the bells, bells, bells, bells—
        Bells, bells, bells—
To the moaning and the groaning of the bells!

KUBLA KHAN

SAMUEL T. COLERIDGE

Kubla Khan was a Chinese prince of the thirteenth century. Coleridge had been reading an old volume about his dynasty, when he fell asleep and dreamed the strange scene and action of this poem. On waking he put into poetry all he could remember of the dream.

In Xanadu did Kubla Khan
A stately pleasure-dome decree:
Where Alph, the sacred river, ran
Through caverns measureless to man,
Down to a sunless sea.
So twice five miles of fertile ground
With walls and towers were girdled round:
And there were gardens bright with sinuous rills
Where blossomed many an incense-bearing tree;
And here were forests ancient as the hills,
Enfolding sunny spots of greenery.

But O! that deep romantic chasm which slanted
Down the green hill athwart a cedarn cover!
A savage place! as holy and enchanted
As e'er beneath a waning moon was haunted
By woman wailing for her demon-lover!
And from this chasm, with ceaseless turmoil seething,
As if this earth in fast thick pants were breathing,
A mighty fountain momently was forced:
Amid whose swift, half-intermitted burst
Huge fragments vaulted like rebounding hail,
Or chaffy grain beneath the thresher's flail:
And 'mid these dancing rocks at once and ever
It flung up momently the sacred river.

Five miles meandering with a mazy motion
Through wood and dale, the sacred river ran,
Then reached the caverns measureless to man,
And sank in tumult to a lifeless ocean:
And 'mid this tumult Kubla heard from far
Ancestral voices prophesying war!

The shadow of the dome of pleasure
Floated midway on the waves;
Where was heard the mingled measure
From the fountain and the caves.
It was a miracle of rare device,
A sunny pleasure-dome with caves of ice!
A damsel with a dulcimer
In a vision once I saw:
It was an Abyssinian maid,
And on her dulcimer she played,
Singing of Mount Abora.
Could I revive within me
Her symphony and song,
To such a deep delight 'twould win me.
That with music loud and long,
I would build that dome in air,
That sunny dome! those caves of ice!
And all who heard should see them there,
And all should cry, Beware! Beware!
His flashing eyes, his floating hair!
Weave a circle round him thrice,
And close your eyes with holy dread,
For he on honey-dew hath fed,
And drunk the milk of Paradise.

THE WONDERER

ROBERT W. SERVICE

I wish that I could understand
The moving marvel of my Hand;
I watch my fingers turn and twist,
The supple bending of my wrist,
The dainty touch of finger-tip,
The steel intensity of grip;
A tool of exquisite design,
With pride I think: "It's mine! It's mine!"

Then there's the wonder of my eyes,
Where hills and houses, seas and skies,
In waves of light converge and pass,
And print themselves as on a glass.
Line, form and color live in me;
I am the Beauty that I see;
Ah! I could write a book of size
About the wonder of my Eyes.

What of the wonder of my Heart,
That plays so faithfully its part?
I hear it running sound and sweet;
It does not seem to miss a beat;
Between the cradle and the grave
It never falters, stanch and brave.
Alas! I wish I had the art
To tell the wonder of my Heart.

Then oh! but how can I explain
The wondrous wonder of my Brain?
That marvelous machine that brings
All consciousness of wonderings;

[235]

That lets me from myself leap out
And watch my body walk about;
It's hopeless—all my words are vain
To tell the wonder of my Brain.

But do not think, O patient friend,
Who reads these stanzas to the end,
That I myself would glorify. . . .
You're just as wonderful as I,
And all creation in our view
Is quite as marvelous as you.
Come, let us on the sea-shore stand
And wonder at a grain of sand;
And then into the meadow pass
And marvel at a blade of grass;
Or cast our vision high and far
And thrill with wonder at a star;
A host of stars—night's holy tent
Huge glittering with wonderment.

If wonder is in great and small,
Then what of Him who made it all?
In eyes and brain and heart and limb
Let's see the wondrous work of Him.
In house and hill and sward and sea,
In bird and beast and flower and tree,
In everything from sun to sod,
The wonder and the awe of God.

Robert W. Service came from Scotland to Canada when he was twenty and spent five years wandering through the wilds and the cities of Canada and the United States. He then became a clerk in a Canadian bank and began to write the wilderness songs that have made him popular. Kipling is his favorite poet and his model. He says, "Kipling comes first with me. He is the greatest of modern writers to my mind. I only wish I could write in his class."

EACH IN HIS OWN TONGUE

WILLIAM HERBERT CARRUTH

A fire-mist and a planet,
   A crystal and a cell,
A jelly-fish and a saurian,
   And caves where the cave-men dwell;
Then a sense of law and beauty
   And a face turned from the clod—
Some call it Evolution,
   And others call it God.

A haze on the far horizon,
   The infinite, tender sky,
The ripe rich tint of the cornfields,
   And the wild geese sailing high—
And all over upland and lowland
   The charm of the golden-rod—
Some of us call it Autumn
   And others call it God.

Like tides on a crescent sea-beach,
   When the moon is new and thin,
Into our hearts high yearnings
   Come welling and surging in—
Come from the mystic ocean,
   Whose rim no foot has trod,—
Some of us call it Longing,
   And others call it God.

A picket frozen on duty,
   A mother starved for her brood,
Socrates drinking the hemlock,
   And Jesus on the rood;

> And millions who, humble and nameless,
>   The straight, hard pathway plod,—
> Some call it Consecration,
>   And others call it God.

SELF-DEPENDENCE

MATTHEW ARNOLD

Weary of myself, and sick of asking
  What I am, and what I ought to be,
At this vessel's prow I stand, which bears me
  Forwards, forwards, o'er the starlit sea.

And a look of passionate desire
  O'er the sea and to the stars I send;
"Ye who from my childhood up have calm'd me,
  Calm me, ah, compose me to the end!

"Ah, once more," I cried, "ye stars, ye waters,
  On my heart your mighty charm renew;
Still, still let me, as I gaze upon you,
  Feel my soul becoming vast like you!"

From the intense, clear, star-sown vault of heaven,
  Over the lit sea's unquiet way,
In the rustling night-air came the answer:
  "Wouldst thou *be* as these are? *Live* as they.

"Unaffrighted by the silence round them,
  Undistracted by the sights they see,
These demand not that the things without them
  Yield them love, amusement, sympathy.

"And with joy the stars perform their shining,
  And the sea its long moon-silver'd roll;

For self-poised they live, nor pine with noting
  All the fever of some differing soul.

"Bounded by themselves, and unregardful
  In what state God's other works may be,
In their own tasks all their powers pouring.
  These attain the mighty life you see."

O air-born voice! long since, severely clear,
A cry like thine in mine own heart I hear:
"Resolve to be thyself; and know that he,
Who finds himself, loses his misery!"

SONNET ON HIS BLINDNESS

JOHN MILTON

Milton was entirely blind for the last twenty years of his life but he went courageously on with his work. He dictated all of his great poem, "Paradise Lost."

When I consider how my light is spent
Ere half my days, in this dark world and wide,
And that one talent, which is death to hide,
Lodged with me useless, though my soul more bent
To serve therewith my Maker, and present
  My true account, lest He, returning, chide:
  "Doth God exact day labor, light denied?"
I fondly ask; but Patience, to prevent
  That murmur, soon replies, "God doth not need
    Either man's work, or His own gifts; who best
    Bear His mild yoke, they serve Him best. His state
Is kingly. Thousands at His bidding speed,
  And post o'er land and ocean without rest;
    They also serve who only stand and wait."

LINES FROM "IN MEMORIAM"

ALFRED TENNYSON

Alfred Tennyson and Arthur Henry Hallam were great friends through their college days at Cambridge. Hallam died suddenly at the age of twenty-two and his loss was a terrible grief to Tennyson. During the next seventeen years Tennyson wrote "In Memoriam" as a tribute to his friend.

Strong Son of God, immortal Love,
    Whom we, that have not seen thy face
    By faith, and faith alone, embrace,
Believing where we cannot prove:

Thine are these orbs of light and shade;
    Thou madest Life in man and brute;
    Thou madest Death; and lo, thy foot
Is on the skull which thou hast made.

Thou wilt not leave us in the dust:
    Thou madest man, he knows not why;
    He thinks he was not made to die;
And thou hast made him; thou art just.

Thou seemest human and divine,
    The highest, holiest manhood, thou;
    Our wills are ours, we know not how;
Our wills are ours, to make them thine.

Our little systems have their day;
    They have their day and cease to be:
    They are but broken lights of thee,
And thou, O Lord, art more than they.

THE DEAF

L. LAMPREY

If we could hear the voice of Lincoln saying,
  "Nothing is settled till it's settled right,"
Would it have power to hold our thoughts from straying
  And lead us toward the light?

If he should stand among us, grave and tender,
  And say, "God must have loved the common men,"
Should we take heed of laborer, ploughman, vender,
  Servant or craftsman then?

If Lincoln moved among us as they knew him
  In that dread spring of eighteen-sixty-five,
Should we pay him the homage that was due him
  While he was yet alive?

None are so deaf as those who will not listen—
  Old is the saying, commonplace and true.
And who are we, that we should boldly christen
  Our day, not theirs, as new?

From *Days of the Leaders, 1925*

(*Lincoln once told a friend of a dream he had had in which he was looking at a great crowd of people, and a bystander said to him that they seemed to be very common folk. "Then," said Lincoln, "I thought I said in my dream, that God must have loved the common people because He made so many of them.*")

CHARTLESS

EMILY DICKINSON

I never saw a moor,
I never saw the sea;
Yet know I how the heather looks,
And what a wave must be.

I never spoke with God,
Nor visited in heaven;
Yet certain am I of the spot
As if the chart were given.

Emily Dickinson was one of the most interesting New England poets. She wrote in the seclusion of her home at Amherst, Mass., and it was not until after her death that her verses were published, and many years more before she became famous.

A VISION

HENRY VAUGHAN

I saw Eternity the other night,
Like a great ring of pure and endless light,
  All calm, as it was bright:—
And round beneath it, Time, in hours, days, years,
  Driven by the spheres,
Like a vast shadow moved; in which the World
  And all her train were hurl'd.

JERUSALEM

WILLIAM BLAKE

And did those feet in ancient time
  Walk upon England's mountains green?
And was the holy Lamb of God
  On England's pleasant pastures seen?

And did the Countenance Divine
  Shine forth upon our clouded hills?
And was Jerusalem builded here
  Among these dark Satanic mills?

Bring me my bow of burning gold!
  Bring me my arrows of desire!
Bring me my spear! O clouds, unfold!
  Bring me my chariot of fire!

I will not cease from mental fight,
  Nor shall my sword sleep in my hand,
Till we have built Jerusalem
  In England's green and pleasant land.

From *Milton*.

FOLLOW THE GLEAM

ALFRED TENNYSON

Not of the sunlight,
Not of the moonlight,
Not of the starlight!
O young Mariner,
Down to the haven,

[243]

Call your companions,
Launch your vessel,
And crowd your canvas,
And, ere it vanishes
Over the margin,
After it, follow it,
Follow The Gleam.

AN ANCIENT PRAYER

THOMAS H. B. WEBB

Give me a good digestion, Lord, and also something to
    digest;
Give me a healthy body, Lord, and sense to keep it at its
    best.
Give me a healthy mind, good Lord, to keep the good and
    pure in sight,
Which, seeing sin, is not appalled, but finds a way to set it
    right.

Give me a mind that is not bound, that does not whimper,
    whine or sigh.
Don't let me worry overmuch about the fussy thing called I.
Give me a sense of humor, Lord; give me the grace to see a
    joke,
To get some happiness from life and pass it on to other folk.

SONG

HARTLEY COLERIDGE

She is not fair to outward view
   As many maidens be,
Her loveliness I never knew
   Until she smiled on me;
O, then I saw her eye was bright,
A well of love, a spring of light!

But now her looks are coy and cold,
   To mine they ne'er reply,
And yet I cease not to behold
   The love-light in her eye;
Her very frowns are fairer far
Than smiles of other maidens are.

A SONNET FROM THE PORTUGUESE

ELIZABETH BARRETT BROWNING

How do I love thee? Let me count the ways.
I love thee to the depth and breadth and height
My soul can reach, when feeling out of sight
For the ends of Being and ideal Grace.
I love thee to the level of everyday's
Most quiet need, by sun and candle-light.
I love thee freely, as men strive for Right;
I love thee purely, as they turn from Praise.
I love thee with the passion put to use
In my old griefs, and with my childhood's faith.

I love thee with a love I seemed to lose
With my lost saints,—I love thee with the breath,
Smiles, tears, of all my life!—and, if God choose,
I shall but love thee better after death.

Read after the torrid love songs so much in vogue in our day, this true love poem (from Sonnets From the Portuguese) by one of the world's greatest lovers, comes like a fresh, clean wind.

BROTHERHOOD

EDWIN MARKHAM

The crest and crowning of all good,
Life's final star, is Brotherhood;
For it will bring again to Earth
Her long-lost Poesy and Mirth;
Will send new light on every face,
A kingly power upon the race.
And till it come, we men are slaves,
And travel downward to the dust of graves.
Come, clear the way, then, clear the way;
Blind creeds and kings have had their day;
Break the dead branches from the path;
Our hope is in the aftermath—
Our hope is in heroic men
Star-led to build the world again.
Make way for Brotherhood—make way for Man!

Edwin Markham became famous in 1899 for a poem entitled "The Man with the Hoe," which voiced a challenge for social justice that went around the world. "Brotherhood" expresses another of the convictions this poet lived for.

PRECIOUS WORDS

EMILY DICKINSON

He ate and drank the precious words.
His spirit grew robust;
He knew no more that he was poor,
Nor that his frame was dust.
He danced along the dingy days,
And this bequest of wings
Was but a book. What liberty
A loosened spirit brings!

GOD'S GRANDEUR

GERARD MANLEY HOPKINS

The world is charged with the grandeur of God.
It will flame out, like shining from shook foil;
It gathers to a greatness, like the ooze of oil
Crushed. Why do men then now not reck his rod?
Generations have trod, have trod, have trod;
And all is seared with trade; bleared, smeared with toil;
And wears man's smudge and shares man's smell: the soil
Is bare now, nor can foot feel, being shod.
And for all this, nature is never spent;
There lives the dearest freshness deep down things;
And though the last lights off the black West went
Oh, morning, at the brown brink eastward, springs—
Because the Holy Ghost over the bent
World broods with warm breast and with ah! bright wings.

From *Poems of Gerard Manley Hopkins Edited by Robert Bridges, Oxford University Press, 1931*

LINES FROM "BYRON"

JOAQUIN MILLER

In men whom men condemn as ill
I find so much of goodness still,
In men whom men pronounce divine
I find so much of sin and blot,
I do not dare to draw a line
Between the two, where God has not.

MIRACLES

WALT WHITMAN

Why, who makes much of a miracle?
As to me I know of nothing else but miracles,
Whether I walk the streets of Manhattan,
Or dart my sight over the roofs of houses toward the sky,
Or wade with naked feet along the beach just in the edge of
    the water,
Or stand under trees in the woods,

   .   .   .   .

Or watch honey-bees busy around the hive of a summer fore-
    noon,
Or animals feeding in the fields,
Or birds, or the wonderfulness of insects in the air,
Or the wonderfulness of the sundown, or of the stars shining
    so quiet and bright,
Or the exquisite delicate thin curve of the new moon in
    spring;
These with the rest, one and all, are to me miracles,
The whole referring, yet each distinct and in its place.

To me every hour of the light and dark is a miracle,
Every cubic inch of space is a miracle,
Every square yard of the surface of the earth is spread with
the same,
Every foot of the interior swarms with the same.

To me the sea is a continual miracle,
The fishes that swim—the rocks—the motion of the waves—
the ships with men in them,
What stranger miracles are there?

I HEAR AMERICA SINGING

WALT WHITMAN

I hear America singing, the varied carols I hear,
Those of mechanics, each one singing his as it should be blithe
and strong,
The carpenter singing his as he measures his plank or beam,
The mason singing his as he makes ready for work, or leaves
off work,
The boatman singing what belongs to him in his boat, the
deckhand singing on the steamboat deck,
The shoemaker singing as he sits on his bench, the hatter
singing as he stands,
The wood-cutter's song, the plowboy's on his way in the
morning, or at noon intermission or at sundown,
The delicious singing of the mother, or of the young wife at
work, or of the girl sewing or washing,
Each singing what belongs to him or her and to none else,
The day what belongs to the day—at night the party of young
fellows, robust, friendly,
Singing with open mouths their strong melodious songs.

RECESSIONAL

RUDYARD KIPLING

In 1897 the sixtieth year of Queen Victoria's reign was celebrated with a great jubilee in England. Kipling wrote this poem in honor of the occasion and it is now recognized as one of the greatest national hymns ever written.

God of our fathers, known of old—
 Lord of our far-flung battle line—
Beneath whose awful hand we hold
 Dominion over palm and pine—
Lord God of Hosts, be with us yet,
Lest we forget—lest we forget!

The tumult and the shouting dies—
 The Captains and the Kings depart—
Still stands Thine ancient sacrifice,
 An humble and a contrite heart.
Lord God of Hosts, be with us yet,
Lest we forget—lest we forget!

Far-called, our navies melt away—
 On dune and headland sinks the fire—
Lo, all our pomp of yesterday
 Is one with Nineveh and Tyre!
Judge of the Nations, spare us yet,
Lest we forget—lest we forget!

If, drunk with sight of power, we loose
 Wild tongues that have not Thee in awe—
Such boasting as the Gentiles use,
 Or lesser breeds without the Law—
Lord God of Hosts, be with us yet,
Lest we forget—lest we forget!

For heathen heart that puts her trust
  In reeking tube and iron shard—
All valiant dust that builds on dust,
  And guarding, calls not Thee to guard,
For frantic boast and foolish word,
  Thy Mercy on Thy People, Lord! Amen!

PLAY THE GAME

HENRY NEWBOLT

There's a breathless hush in the Close tonight—
  Ten to make and the match to win—
A bumping pitch and a blinding light,
  An hour to play and the last man in.
And it's not for the sake of a ribboned coat,
  Or the selfish hope of a season's fame,
But his Captain's hand on his shoulder smote—
  "Play up! Play up! and play the game!"

The sand of the desert is sodden red,—
  Red with the wreck of a square that broke;—
The Gatling's jammed and the Colonel dead,
  And the regiment blind with dust and smoke.
The river of death has brimmed his banks,
  And England's far and Honor a name,
But the voice of a schoolboy rallies the ranks;
  "Play up! play up! and play the game!"

This is the word that year by year,
  While in her place the School is set,
Every one of her sons must hear,
  And none that hears it dare forget.
  This they all with a joyful mind
  Bear through life like a torch of flame,
And falling fling to the host behind—
  "Play up! play up! and play the game!"

LINES FROM "SONG OF MYSELF"

WALT WHITMAN

A child said, *"What is the grass?"* fetching it to me with
full hands;
How could I answer the child? I do not know what it is any-
more than he.

. . . .

I believe a leaf of grass is no less than the journey-work of
the stars,
And the pismire is equally perfect, and a grain of sand, and
the egg of the wren,
And the tree-toad is a chef-d'oeuvre for the highest,
And the running blackberry would adorn the parlours of
heaven,
And the narrowest hinge in my hand puts to scorn all ma-
chinery,
And the cow crunching with depress'd head surpasses any
statue,
And a mouse is miracle enough to stagger sextillions of in-
fidels.

*Walt Whitman loved America and American people in every walk
of life. He believed in democracy and sang of it and the common man's
part in it. His first book of poems, "Leaves of Grass," was published in
1855 and raised a storm of protest and censure. But with the years it has
assumed its place and is thought by many critics to have been, since then,
the greatest force in American poetry.*

THE MARSHES OF GLYNN

SIDNEY LANIER

Sidney Lanier, a southern poet, was a soldier in the Confederate Army during the Civil War. He loved two things—his flute, and Nature, and most of his poems are about the woods and marshes, or about music. The verses that follow are part of a long poem describing the poet's day spent in the woods, to step forth at sunset on the water marshes of Glynn.

To the edge of the wood I am drawn, I am drawn,
Where the gray beach glimmering runs, as a belt of the dawn,
   For a mete and a mark
      To the forest-dark:—
        So:
Affable live-oak, leaning low,—
Thus—with your favor—soft, with a reverent hand
(Not lightly touching your person, Lord of the land!),
Bending your beauty aside, with a step I stand
On the firm-packed sand,
      Free
By a world of marsh that borders a world of sea.

Sinuous southward and sinuous northward the shimmer-
    ing band
Of the sand-beach fastens the fringe of the marsh to the
    folds of the land.
Inward and outward to northward and southward the beach-
    lines linger and curl
As a silver-wrought garment that clings to and follows the
    firm sweet limbs of a girl.

Vanishing, swerving, evermore curving again into sight,
Softly the sand-beach wavers away to a dim gray looping of
    light.

And what if behind me to westward the wall of the woods
  stands high?
The world lies east: how ample, the marsh and the sea and
  the sky!
A league and a league of marsh-grass, waist-high, broad in
  the blade,
Green, and all of a height, and unflecked with a light or a
  shade,
Stretch leisurely off, in a pleasant plain,
To the terminal blue of the main.

Oh, what is abroad in the marsh and the terminal sea?
  Somehow my soul seems suddenly free
From the weighing of fate and the sad discussion of sin,
By the length and the breadth and the sweep of the marshes
  of Glynn.

Ye marshes, how candid and simple and nothing-withholding
  and free
Ye publish yourselves to the sky and offer yourselves to the
  sea!
Tolerant plains, that suffer the sea and the rains and the sun,
Ye spread and span like the catholic man who hath mightily
  won
God out of knowledge and good out of infinite pain
And sight out of blindness and purity out of a stain.

As the marsh-hen secretly builds on the watery sod,
Behold I will build me a nest on the greatness of God:
I will fly in the greatness of God as the marsh-hen flies
In the freedom that fills all the space 'twixt the marsh and the
  skies:
By so many roots as the marsh-grass sends in the sod
I will heartily lay me a-hold on the greatness of God:
Oh, like to the greatness of God is the greatness within
The range of the marshes, the liberal marshes of Glynn.

And the sea lends large, as the marsh: lo, out of his plenty
    the sea
Pours fast: full soon the time of the flood-tide must be:
Look how the grace of the sea doth go
About and about through the intricate channels that flow
    Here and there,
        Everywhere,
Till his waters have flooded the uttermost creeks and the
    low-lying lanes,
And the marsh is meshed with a million veins,
That like as with rosy and silvery essences flow
In the rose-and-silver evening glow.

        Farewell, my lord Sun!
The creeks overflow: a thousand rivulets run
'Twixt the roots of the sod; the blades of the marsh-grass
    stir;
Passeth a hurrying sound of wings that westward whirr;
Passeth, and all is still; and the currents cease to run;
And the sea and the marsh are one.
How still the plains of the waters be!
The tide is his ecstasy.
The tide is at his highest height:
        And it is night.

And now from the Vast of the Lord will the waters of sleep
Roll in on the souls of men,
But who will reveal to our waking ken
The forms that swim and the shapes that creep
        Under the waters of sleep?
And I would I could know what swimmeth below when the
    tide comes in
On the length and breadth of the marvelous marshes of
    Glynn.

THE MAN OF PRAYER

CHRISTOPHER SMART

Strong is the horse upon his speed;
Strong in pursuit the rapid glede,
   Which makes at once his game:
Strong the tall ostrich on the ground;
Strong through the turbulent profound
   Shoots xiphias to his aim.

Strong is the lion—like a coal
His eyeball—like a bastion's mole
   His chest against the foes:
Strong, the gier-eagle on his sail,
Strong against tide, th' enormous whale
   Emerges as he goes.

But stronger still, in earth and air,
And in the sea, the man of prayer,
   And far beneath the tide:
And in the seat to faith assigned,
Where ask is have, where seek is find,
   Where knock is open wide.

THE ARROW AND THE SONG

HENRY W. LONGFELLOW

I shot an arrow into the air,
It fell to earth, I know not where;
For, so swiftly it flew, the sight
Could not follow it in its flight.

I breathed a song into the air,
   It fell to earth, I know not where;
For who has sight so keen and strong
   That it can follow the flight of song?

Long, long afterward, in an oak
   I found the arrow, still unbroke;
And the song, from beginning to end,
   I found again in the heart of a friend.

ALADDIN

JAMES RUSSELL LOWELL

When I was a beggarly boy,
   And lived in a cellar damp,
I had not a friend nor a toy,
   But I had Aladdin's lamp;
When I could not sleep for cold,
   I had fire enough in my brain,
And builded, with roofs of gold,
   My beautiful castles in Spain!

Since then I have toiled day and night,
   I have money and power good store,
But I'd give all my lamps of silver bright,
   For the one that is mine no more;
Take, Fortune, whatever you choose,
   You gave, and may snatch again;
I have nothing 't would pain me to lose,
   For I own no more castles in Spain!

HISTORY

RALPH WALDO EMERSON

There is no great and no small
To the Soul that maketh all:
And where it cometh, all things are;
And it cometh every where.

I am owner of the sphere,
Of the seven stars and the solar year,
Of Caesar's hand, and Plato's brain,
Of Lord Christ's heart, and Shakespeare's strain.

"I'M NOBODY! WHO ARE YOU?"

EMILY DICKINSON

I'm nobody! Who are you?
Are you nobody, too?
Then there's a pair of us—don't tell!
They'd banish us, you know.

How dreary to be somebody!
How public, like a frog
To tell your name the livelong day
To an admiring bog!

ONCE IN A SAINTLY PASSION

JAMES THOMSON

Once in a saintly passion
I cried with desperate grief,
"O Lord, my heart is black with guile,
Of sinners I am chief."

[258]

Then stooped my guardian angel
And whispered from behind,
"Vanity, my little man,
You're nothing of the kind."

FLOWER IN THE CRANNIED WALL

ALFRED TENNYSON

Flower in the crannied wall,
I pluck you out of the crannies,
I hold you here, root and all, in my hand,
Little flower—but *if* I could understand
What you are, root and all, and all in all,
I should know what God and man is.

PILGRIMAGE

SIR WALTER RALEIGH

Give me my scallop-shell of quiet,
My staff of faith to walk upon,
My scrip of joy, immortal diet,
My bottle of salvation,
My gown of glory, hope's true gage,
And thus I'll take my pilgrimage.

THE EXPRESS

STEPHEN SPENDER

After the first powerful plain manifesto
The black statement of pistons, without more fuss
But gliding like a queen, she leaves the station.
Without bowing and with restrained unconcern
She passes the houses which humbly crowd outside,
The gasworks and at last the heavy page
Of death, printed by gravestones in the cemetery.
Beyond the town there lies the open country
Where, gathering speed, she acquires mystery,
The luminous self-possession of ships on ocean.
It is now she begins to sing—at first quite low
Then loud, and at last with a jazzy madness—
The song of her whistle screaming at curves,
Of deafening tunnels, brakes, innumerable bolts.
And always light, aerial, underneath
Goes the elate meter of her wheels.
Steaming through metal landscape on her lines
She plunges new eras of wild happiness
Where speed throws up strange shapes, broad curves
And parallels clean like the steel of guns.
At last, further than Edinburgh or Rome,
Beyond the crest of the world, she reaches night
Where only a low streamline brightness
Of phosphorus on the tossing hills is white.
Ah, like a comet through flames she moves entranced
Wrapt in her music no bird song, no, nor bough
Breaking with honey buds, shall ever equal.

THE PEOPLE, YES

CARL SANDBURG

The people, yes, the people,
Until the people are taken care of one way or another,
Until the people are solved somehow for the day and hour,
Until then one hears "Yes but the people what about the
    people?"
Sometimes as though the people is a child to be pleased or
    fed
Or again a hoodlum you have to be tough with
And seldom as though the people is a caldron and a reservoir
Of the human reserves that shape history,
The river of welcome wherein the broken First Families
    fade,
The great pool wherein wornout breeds and clans drop for
    restorative silence.

Fire, chaos, shadows,
Events trickling from a thin line of flame
On into cries and combustions never expected:
The people have the element of surprise.
    Where are the kings today?
What has become of their solid and fastened thrones?
Who are the temporary puppets holding sway while any-
    thing,
    "God only knows what," waits around a corner, sits in the
        shadows and holds an ax, waiting for the appointed
        hour?

"The czar has eight million men with guns and bayonets.
"Nothing can happen to the czar.
"The czar is the voice of God and shall live forever.
"Turn and look at the forest of steel and cannon
"Where the czar is guarded by eight million soldiers,

"Nothing can happen to the czar."

They said that for years and in the summer of 1914
In the Year of Our Lord Nineteen Hundred and Fourteen
As a portent and an assurance they said with owl faces:
    "Nothing can happen to the czar."
Yet the czar and his bodyguard of eight million vanished
And the czar stood in a cellar before a little firing squad
And the command of fire was given
And the czar stepped into regions of mist and ice
The czar travelled into an ethereal uncharted siberia
While two kaisers also vanished from thrones
Ancient and established in blood and iron—
Two kaisers backed by ten million bayonets
Had their crowns in a gutter, their palaces mobbed.
    In fire, chaos, shadows,
In hurricanes beyond foretelling of probabilities,
In the shove and whirl of unforeseen combustions
    The people, yes, the people,
Move eternally in the elements of surprise,
Changing from hammer to bayonet and back to hammer,
The hallelujah chorus forever shifting its star soloists.

PSALM ONE HUNDRED TWENTY-ONE

KING DAVID

I will lift up mine eyes unto the hills,
From whence cometh my help.
My help cometh from the Lord,
Which made heaven and earth.
He will not suffer thy foot to be moved;
He that keepeth thee will not slumber.
Behold, he that keepeth Israel
Shall neither slumber nor sleep.

The Lord is thy keeper;
The Lord is thy shade upon thy right hand.
The sun shall not smite thee by day,
Nor the moon by night.
The Lord shall preserve thee from all evil;
He shall preserve thy soul.
The Lord shall preserve thy going out and thy coming in
From this time forth, and even for evermore.

THE MYSTERY OF DEATH

THE APOSTLE PAUL

Behold, I show you a mystery;
We shall not all sleep, but we shall all be changed, in a moment, in the twinkling of an eye, at the last trump:
For the trumpet shall sound, and the dead shall be raised incorruptible, and we shall be changed.
For this corruptible must put on incorruption,
And this mortal must put on immortality.
So when this corruptible shall have put on incorruption,
And this mortal shall have put on immortality.
Then shall be brought to pass the saying that is written,
"Death is swallowed up in victory.
O death, where is thy sting?
O grave, where is thy victory?"
The sting of death is sin; and the strength of sin is the law.
But thanks be to God,
Which giveth us the victory through our Lord Jesus Christ.
Therefore, my beloved brethren, be ye steadfast, unmovable,
Always abounding in the work of the Lord,
Forasmuch as ye know that your labour is not in vain in the Lord.

From *I Corinthians, Chapter 15*

"THEY THAT GO DOWN . . ."

PSALM 107: VERSES 23–31

They that go down to the sea in ships, that do business in
  great waters;
These see the works of the Lord, and his wonders in the
  deep.
For he commandeth, and raiseth the stormy wind,
Which lifteth up the waves thereof.
They mount up to heaven, they go down again to the depths:
Their soul is melted because of trouble.
They reel to and fro, and stagger like a drunken man,
And are at their wits' end.
Then they cry unto the Lord in their trouble,
And he bringeth them out of their distresses.
He maketh the storm a calm, so that the waves thereof are
  still.
Then are they glad because they be quiet;
So he bringeth them unto their desired haven.
Oh that men would praise the Lord for his goodness,
And for his wonderful works to the children of men!

INDEX

NAMES OF POETS IN CAPS.

Titles of Poems, caps and lower case, roman.

Opening lines or phrases in italics, caps and lower case.

INDEX

[266]

Index

Index

Index